■ PEOPLES OF AFRICA ■

# PEOPLES OF SOUTHERN AFRICA

THE DIAGRAM GROUP

Facts On File, Inc.

**Peoples of Africa: Peoples of Southern Africa**

**Diagram Visual Information Ltd**

| | |
|---|---|
| *Editorial director:* | Bridget Giles |
| *Contributors:* | Trevor Day, Theodore Rowland Entwistle, David Lambert, Keith Lye, Oliver Marshall, Christopher Priest |
| *Editors:* | Margaret Doyle, Moira Johnston, Ian Wood |
| *Indexer:* | David Harding |
| *Art director/designer:* | Philip Patenall |
| *Artists:* | Chris Allcott, Darren Bennett, Bob Garwood, Elsa Godfrey, Brian Hewson, Kyri Kyriacou, Janos Marffy, Kathy McDougall, Patrick Mulrey, Rob Shone, Graham Rosewarne, Peter Ross |
| *Production director:* | Richard Hummerstone |
| *Production:* | Mark Carry, Lee Lawrence, Ollie Madden, Philip Richardson, Dave Wilson |
| *Research director:* | Matt Smout |
| *Researchers:* | Pamela Kea, Chris Owens, Catherine Michard, Neil McKenna |

*With the assistance of:*
Dr Elizabeth Dunstan, International African Institute, School of Oriental and African Studies, University of London
David Hall, African studies bibliographer at the School of Oriental and African Studies, University of London
Horniman Museum, London
Museum of Mankind library, British Museum
Survival International
WWF-UK

Facts On File Inc.
11 Penn Plaza
New York NY 10001

**Library of Congress Cataloging-in-Publication Data**

Peoples of Southern Africa / the Diagram Group.
    p.    cm. – (Peoples of Africa)
    Includes index.
    ISBN 0-8160-3487-7 (alk. paper)
    1. Ethnology–Africa, Southern. 2. Africa, Southern–Social life and customs. I. Diagram Group. II. Series: Peoples of Africa (New York, N.Y.)
GN656.P46   1997
305.8'00968–dc20                        96-38736

Facts On File books are available at special discounts when purchased in bulk quantities for businesses, associations, institutions, or sales promotions. Please call our Special Sales Department in New York at 212/967-8800 or 800/322-8755.

Cover design by Molly Heron

Printed in the United States of America

RRD DIAG 10 9 8 7 6 5 4 3 2 1

This book is printed on acid-free paper

# Contents

Foreword      4–5

## THE REGION

Southern Africa today      6–7
Land      8–9
Climate      10–11
Vegetation      12–13
Wildlife      14–15
Chronology      16–21
Pictorial history      22–23
Distribution of peoples      24–25

## THE PEOPLES

*Peoples pages are in bold; special features are in italic*

**Introduction**      **26–29**
**Afrikaners**      30–35
*The rise and fall of apartheid*      36–41
**Cape Coloreds and Cape Malays**      42–43
**Herero**      44–47
**Indian South Africans**      48–51
**Khoisan**      52–55
**Madagascan peoples**      56–61
*Music: jazz, roots, and mbira*      62–63
**Ndebele and Matabele**      64–67
**Ovambo**      68–71
**Shona**      72–75
*The abandoned civilization of Great Zimbabwe*      76–77
**Sotho**      78–81
**Swazi**      82–85
**Tswana**      86–89
**Venda**      90–93
**Xhosa**      94–97
**Zulu**      98–101
*The Mfecane/Difaqane*      102–103

Appendix: Southern African Languages      104–105
Glossary      106–109
Index      110–112

# Foreword

*Peoples of Southern Africa*, the fifth volume in the Facts On File *Peoples of Africa* series, focuses on the historical and cultural richness of the south of the continent. This area covers the modern nations of Botswana, Lesotho, Mozambique, Namibia, South Africa, Swaziland, and Zimbabwe. The island nations of Comoros, Madagascar, and Mauritius, off the east coast, are also part of this region.

*Inside this volume the reader will find:*

- **The region:** preliminary pages describing in depth the region – its land, climate, vegetation, and wildlife – and others providing a broad historical overview and a current political profile of the whole of Southern Africa.
- **The people:** profiles of more than seventeen major ethnic groups within Southern Africa, describing the **history, language, ways of life, social structure,** and **culture and religion** of each group. A map has been included for each ethnic group to show the general region a group inhabits or is most concentrated in. The people profiles are arranged alphabetically. They are not intended to be encyclopedic; instead, they highlight particular aspects of a culture, focusing on fascinating details that will remain with the reader.
- **Special features:** tinted pages interspersed throughout the volume, each on a particular historical or cultural topic. Historical theme spreads, such as that on Great Zimbabwe describe some of the most interesting periods of Southern African history. Other features, such as that on apartheid, illustrate the way one country's policies can affect the lives of not only South Africans but the citizens of the whole of Southern African. Another feature illustrates the great variety to be found in cultural aspects such as music.
- **Language appendix:** a diagrammatic outline of the African language families, which can be used to locate the languages of the peoples profiled and to see how they relate to other African languages.
- **Glossary and index:** following the profiles, features, and appendix are a comprehensive glossary defining the unfamiliar terms used within the volume and a complete index to the volume. Words that appear in the glossary have been printed in roman in special features and *italics* elsewhere.

Taken as a whole, *Peoples of Southern Africa* is intended to project a living portrait of the region that, with the other volumes in the series, provides the reader with a memorable snapshot of Africa as a place of rich heritage, far-reaching influence, and ongoing cultural diversity.

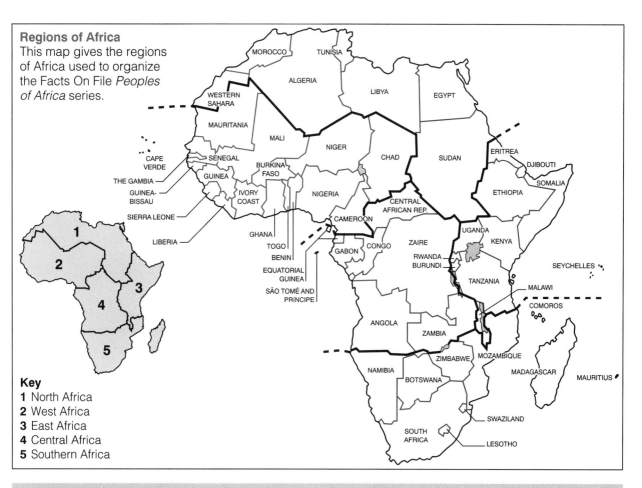

**Regions of Africa**
This map gives the regions of Africa used to organize the Facts On File *Peoples of Africa* series.

MOROCCO
TUNISIA
ALGERIA
LIBYA
EGYPT
WESTERN SAHARA
MAURITANIA
MALI
NIGER
CHAD
SUDAN
ERITREA
DJIBOUTI
SOMALIA
ETHIOPIA
CAPE VERDE
SENEGAL
THE GAMBIA
GUINEA
GUINEA-BISSAU
SIERRA LEONE
BURKINA FASO
IVORY COAST
NIGERIA
CENTRAL AFRICAN REP.
CAMEROON
UGANDA
KENYA
GHANA
TOGO
BENIN
EQUATORIAL GUINEA
SÃO TOMÉ AND PRÍNCIPE
LIBERIA
GABON
CONGO
ZAIRE
RWANDA
BURUNDI
TANZANIA
SEYCHELLES
MALAWI
COMOROS
ANGOLA
ZAMBIA
ZIMBABWE
MOZAMBIQUE
MADAGASCAR
MAURITIUS
NAMIBIA
BOTSWANA
SWAZILAND
SOUTH AFRICA
LESOTHO

**Key**
**1** North Africa
**2** West Africa
**3** East Africa
**4** Central Africa
**5** Southern Africa

**A word about ethnic groups**

The series *Peoples of Africa* focuses on ethnic groups or peoples, useful but difficult-to-define terms. In the past, the word "tribe" was used to describe ethnic groupings, but this is today considered an offensive and arbitrary label. It is incorrect to refer to a group of people who may number in the hundreds of thousands and who have a long history of nation building as a tribe. "Tribe" is now generally used only to describe a basic political unit that exists within some larger ethnic groups, not to describe the group itself. So what is an ethnic group? An ethnic group is distinct from race or nationality; the former is rarely used today because it requires broad and inaccurate generalizations; and the latter describes only the national boundaries within which a person is born or lives. Both categories are fraught with difficulty. For the purposes of this series, the term "ethnic group" is used to describe people who have a common language, history, religion, and cultural and artistic heritage; they may also have a common way of life and often live within the same geographical area.

There are probably more than a thousand ethnic groups in all of Africa. Many are related to one another, often in complex ways. Groups have subgroups and even sub-subgroups. Intermarriage, colonialism, conquest, and migration through the ages have led to many combinations and to an intermixing of influences. In our series we have chosen to focus on only a fraction of Africa's many ethnic groups. A number of factors – including population figures, available information, and recognition outside Africa – were used in making the selection. To a certain extent, however, it was an arbitrary choice, but one that we hope offers a vibrant picture of the people of this continent.

# Southern Africa today

South Africa, Africa's most powerful and wealthiest nation, has dominated Southern Africa for many years. It occupied Namibia from 1915 – illegally from 1969 – until 1990 and supported rebel forces in Mozambique and Angola. South Africa also aided the white-minority regime in Rhodesia until that country became independent as Zimbabwe in 1980. Landlocked Botswana, Lesotho, and Swaziland depend almost totally on South African goodwill. South Africa's intervention in the affairs of its neighbors was part of a destabilizing strategy aimed at preserving its system of racial segregation known as *apartheid*. Since 1994, however, the government of Nelson Mandela has sought to replace racial hatred with reconciliation, while in other parts of Africa the country has begun to act as a mediator in disputes. The new South Africa faces great problems arising from the inequalities of apartheid. In 1993, the white population controlled about eighty-eight percent of the country's wealth, while almost half of the people of South Africa lived below subsistence level with a family income of less than US $200 per month. Other countries in Southern Africa with relatively high per capita (for each person) gross national products (GNPs) are mineral-rich Botswana, one of Africa's most stable democracies, and Namibia. The poorest countries are Mozambique and Madagascar, whose economies are based on *subsistence agriculture*. Mozambique's economy has been shattered by both civil war and *drought*.

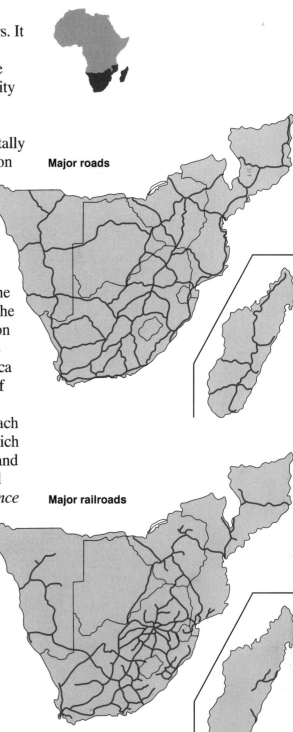

**Major roads**

**Major railroads**

| Country | Population (1994: 000s) | Area (sq. mi) | Per capita GNP (1994: US$) |
|---|---|---|---|
| Botswana | 1,400 | 224,468 | 2,800 |
| Comoros | 485 | 719 | 560 |
| Lesotho | 1,899 | 11,720 | 720 |
| Madagascar | 13,100 | 226,658 | 200 |
| Mauritius | 1,111 | 788 | 3,150 |
| Mozambique | 15,500 | 309,496 | 90 |
| Namibia | 1,565 | 318,261 | 1,970 |
| South Africa | 40,500 | 473,290 | 3,040 |
| Swaziland | 906 | 6,704 | 1,100 |
| Zimbabwe | 10.800 | 150,873 | 500 |

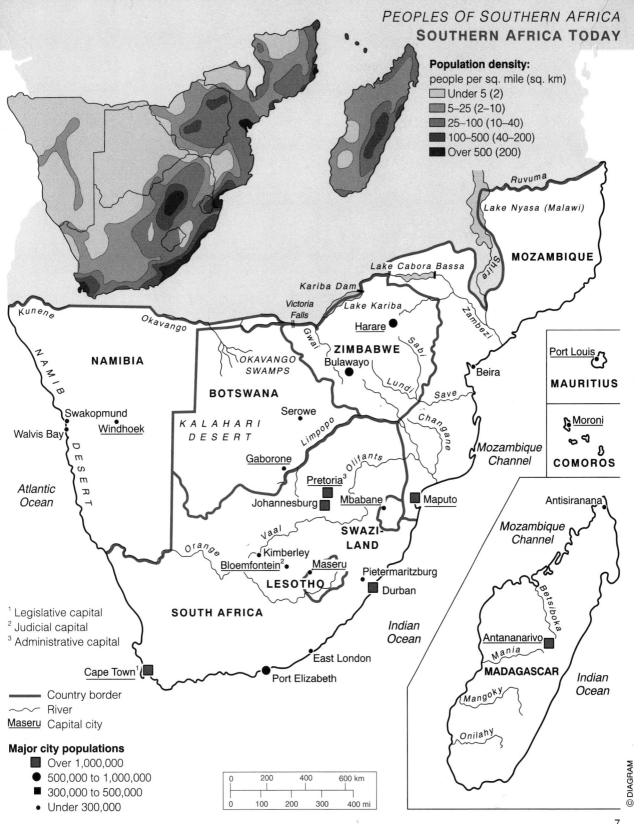

**Population density:**
people per sq. mile (sq. km)
Under 5 (2)
5–25 (2–10)
25–100 (10–40)
100–500 (40–200)
Over 500 (200)

*Ruvuma*

*Lake Nyasa (Malawi)*

**MOZAMBIQUE**

*Shire*

*Lake Cabora Bassa*

Kariba Dam

*Victoria Falls*

*Lake Kariba*

*Zambezi*

Harare ●

**ZIMBABWE**

*Gwai*

Bulawayo ●

*Sabi*

● Beira

*Lundi*

*Save*

*Kunene*

*Okavango*

**NAMIBIA**

*OKAVANGO SWAMPS*

**BOTSWANA**

*Changane*

*Mozambique Channel*

Port Louis 🗺

**MAURITIUS**

🗺 Moroni

**COMOROS**

Swakopmund ●

Serowe ●

*KALAHARI DESERT*

*Limpopo*

Walvis Bay

● Windhoek

**N A M I B   D E S E R T**

*Atlantic Ocean*

Gaborone

*Olifants*

Pretoria[3] ■
Johannesburg ■

Mbabane ●

■ Maputo

Antisiranana ●

*Mozambique Channel*

*Betsiboka*

*Vaal*

**SWAZI-LAND**

*Orange*

● Kimberley

Bloemfontein[2] ●

Maseru ●

Pietermaritzburg ●

**LESOTHO**

■ Durban

*Indian Ocean*

Antananarivo ■

*Mania*

**SOUTH AFRICA**

**MADAGASCAR**

*Indian Ocean*

[1] Legislative capital
[2] Judicial capital
[3] Administrative capital

*Mangoky*

*Onilahy*

East London ●

Cape Town[1] ■

● Port Elizabeth

― Country border
⌇ River
Maseru Capital city

**Major city populations**
■ Over 1,000,000
● 500,000 to 1,000,000
■ 300,000 to 500,000
• Under 300,000

| 0 | 200 | 400 | 600 km |

| 0 | 100 | 200 | 300 | 400 mi |

© DIAGRAM

7

# Land

Southern Africa is bordered by the Atlantic Ocean to the west and the Indian Ocean to the south and east. About 250 miles (400 km) east of the mainland is the world's fourth largest island, Madagascar. Southern Africa consists mainly of ancient igneous (volcanic) rocks overlaid by more recent volcanic and sedimentary rocks. Sand covers much of the northwest. Minerals include large deposits of gold, diamonds, and copper. Much of mainland Southern Africa is a flat upland with troughs and valleys through which the region's chief

## Southern Plateau

The Southern Plateau dominates Southern Africa. In Botswana, eastern Namibia, and Zimbabwe it stands at 3,000–5,000 ft (900–1,500 m). In South Africa, the Southern Plateau has three main divisions: the Middleveld, which is largely under 4,000 ft (1,200 m); the Highveld, most of which is 4,000–6,000 ft (1,200–1,800 m); and the rolling Transvaal Basin, which is mostly below 3,500 ft (1,000 m). Central Madagascar lies mostly between 2,000 and 4,000 ft (600–1,200 m) above sea level. The narrow Caprivi Strip between Angola (in Central Africa) and Namibia is a legacy of the colonial era. The strip was ceded by British Bechuanaland (modern Botswana) to the German colony of South West Africa (present-day Namibia) in order to give them access to the waters of the Zambezi River.

☐ Plateau land below 4,500 ft (1,400 m)
▨ Plateau land above 4,500 ft (1,400 m)

*Caprivi Strip*

*SOUTHERN PLATEAU* *Transvaal Basin*

*Middleveld* *Highveld*

*Atlantic Ocean*

*Indian Ocean*

## Highlands

A series of mountains and cliffs called the Great Escarpment forms the Southern Plateau's raised edge. It includes ranges in Zimbabwe, South Africa, and Lesotho. In Namibia, the Great Escarpment separates the Southern Plateau from the Namib Desert. The greatest heights – over 10,000 ft (3,000 m)– are reached in the Drakensberg Mountains of eastern South Africa and Lesotho. At 11,425 ft (3,482 m), Lesotho's Thabana Ntlenyana is the tallest peak in Southern Africa. Lesotho is almost completely mountainous, the only plains lie in the west. The Cape Mountains are in the southwest of South Africa between the Great Escarpment and the coastal strip. Madagascar's central highlands are mostly the remains of a plateau now deeply dissected by rivers.

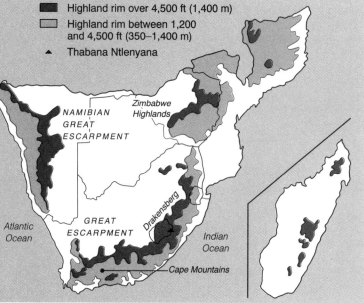

■ Highland rim over 4,500 ft (1,400 m)
☐ Highland rim between 1,200 and 4,500 ft (350–1,400 m)
▲ Thabana Ntlenyana

*NAMIBIAN GREAT ESCARPMENT*

*Zimbabwe Highlands*

*GREAT ESCARPMENT*

*Drakensberg*

*Atlantic Ocean*

*Indian Ocean*

*Cape Mountains*

rivers flow. West, south, and east of this plateau, a raised rim – the Great Escarpment – reaches 11,000 ft (3,300 m) high. From this mountainous area, cliffs and steep slopes lead down to either coastal plains or the sea. Madagascar has a central "spine" of highlands that reach up to 9,000 ft (2,700 m) high with coastal lowlands to the west and east. Throughout region, most people live on fertile plateaus or coastal areas, especially in the south and east of the mainland.

### Coastal lowlands

The shores of mainland Southern Africa lack large inlets and peninsulas. Madagascar's east coast is also very straight. There are some good natural harbors, however, especially Table Bay and Algoa Bay in South Africa, and Maputo Bay in Mozambique. Much of the shoreline is low, with sandy beaches, swamps, and lagoons in Mozambique and farms farther inland. The coastal plain covers most of southern Mozambique and a wide coastal plain occupies western Madagascar. South Africa's southern shore is rocky where mountains come close to the sea. On the Atlantic coast, huge sand dunes dominate the arid Namibian shoreline where the Namib Desert meets the sea.

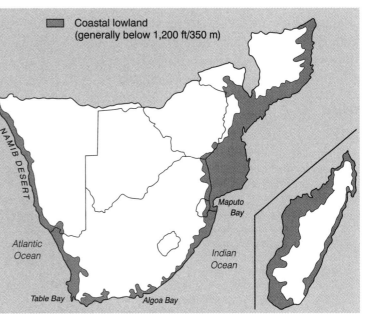

Coastal lowland (generally below 1,200 ft/350 m)

### Rivers and lakes

The longest of the many rivers that flow into the Indian Ocean are the Zambezi and Limpopo. The Zambezi flows between Zambia and Zimbabwe, plunging over the Victoria Falls before entering Mozambique, where its valley forms the southern tip of the Great Rift Valley – a depression that extends from the Jordan River Valley in southwest Asia right across East Africa. The Kariba and Cabora Bassa dams on the Zambezi have created two huge, artificial lakes: Lake Kariba and Lake Cabora Bassa. The Orange River is the longest of the few rivers to reach the Atlantic. One river never enters the sea at all: the Okavango splits up into streams (the Okavango Delta) in northeast Botswana and forms the vast, marshy Okavango Swamps – the world's largest inland delta (river mouth).

© DIAGRAM

# Climate

Southern Africa lies south of the equator but only its northernmost regions lie inside the tropics. Therefore, the region has a wide variety of climates. Eastern Madagascar has a tropical wet climate and is always warm with rain all year round. Much of Mozambique, Zimbabwe, and Madagascar have a tropical wet and dry climate – they are always warm and have both rainy and dry seasons. Much of Namibia and Botswana, western parts of Zimbabwe and South Africa, and southwest Madagascar are arid or semiarid, with large temperature swings between day and night and low annual rainfall. Drier still is the desert climate of southern and western Namibia and western South Africa. The Drakensberg Mountains, however, are cool and moist. South Africa's southeast coast has a subtropical moist climate – hot, humid summers and dry, sunny winters – and its southwest tip has warm, dry summers and mild, moist winters.

### Winds

From November through April, winds blow roughly clockwise around a low-pressure air mass that covers most of Africa south of the equator. This means that air flows mainly south or southwest down the east coast of Southern Africa and over Madagascar, but mainly north up the Atlantic side of the region. There is only light air movement over most of the land in between. From May through October, winds blow outward from a small high-pressure center over South Africa but inward toward a great low-pressure air mass that covers most of Africa north of the equator. This attracts an airflow that travels northwest across northern parts of the Southern African mainland and Madagascar.

### Temperature

Temperature depends largely on altitude and distance from the equator. The tropical coasts of Mozambique and Madagascar are hot all year round, with average temperatures of between 21 and 27 °C (70 and 80 °F). Farther from the equator, temperatures tend to be lower and cover a greater range. Cape Town's monthly average ranges from 22 °C (71 °F) in January and February to 13 °C (55 °F) in July. Some uplands have much greater extremes. Botswana can exceed 38 °C (100 °F) in summer but in winter frosts form and snow falls on high plateaus and peaks of South Africa and Lesotho. Chilly seawater keeps much of the Atlantic coast a cool 10–16 °C (50–60 °F) all the year.

### Rainfall

In most of the region rain falls mainly in the summer, but summers are dry and winters wet in the extreme south west. Rainfall is greatest near the Indian Ocean. The Madagascan capital Antananarivo receives 128 in. (325 cm) a year. Namibia's Atlantic coast gets the least rain. Parts of the Namib Desert, along the western coast of Southern Africa, receive less than 1 in. (2.5 cm) of rainfall a year. Offshore in the Atlantic, the strong, northward-flowing Benguela Current chills the air, producing fogs but little rain. Much of inland Southern Africa has under 30 in. (76 cm) of rain a year. In fact, only one third of South Africa's farmland has enough rain to make growing crops easy.

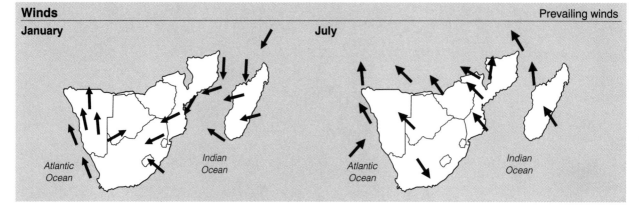

**Winds** — Prevailing winds

January — July

Atlantic Ocean — Indian Ocean

## Temperature

Actual surface temperature

### January

■ 15–20 °C (59–68 °F)
■ 20–25 °C (68–77 °F)

■ 25–30 °C (77–86 °F)

■ 30–35 °C (86–95 °F)
■ Above 35 °C (95 °F)

### July

□ Below 5 °C (41 °F)
■ 5–10 °C (41–50 °F)

■ 10–15 °C (50–59 °F)

■ 15–20 °C (59–68 °F)
■ 20–25 °C (68–77 °F)

## Rainfall

Total rainfall

### November to April

□ Below 5 in. (13 cm)
■ 5–10 in. (13–25 cm)

■ 10–20 in. (25–51 cm)

■ 20–40 in. (51–102 cm)
■ Above 40 in. (102 cm)

### May to October

□ Below 5 in. (13 cm)

■ 5–10 in. (13–25 cm)

■ 10–20 in. (25–51 cm)
■ Above 20 in. (51 cm)

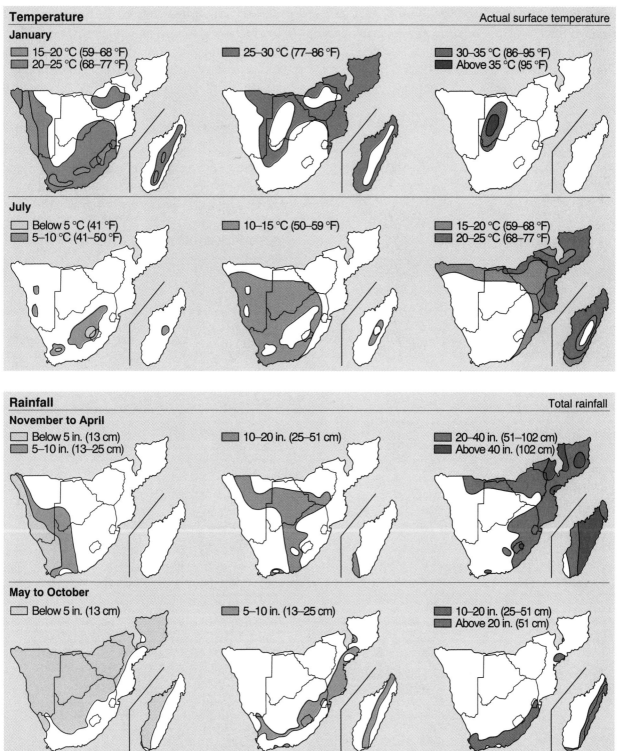

# Vegetation

Southern Africa generally has too little rain to support thick forests. Much of the north is open woodland with trees of only moderate height. Prairie grasses cover eastern South Africa's Highveld and *drought*-resistant plants occur in the deserts and semideserts of the west, southwest, and center. The Kalahari Desert is not considered to be a true desert by some experts as parts of it have relatively high rainfall. Although the Kalahari's southwest is covered by

## Desert and semidesert

**Typical plants**
1 Red hot poker
2 Elephant's trunk
3 Stone plant

The Namib Desert is the oldest desert in the world and has the highest sand dunes in the world. Sand dunes line the coast and gravel plains occur inland. Few plants grow in the Namib except for some specialized, cactuslike plants and hardy species such as acacia trees. The kokerboom (or quiver tree) is an aloe that has a trunk which bears a canopy of swordlike leaves. The elephant's trunk (or half-mens) has a spiky pillar that is crowned with leaves. Welwitschia plants have only two long, leaves that get split into ribbons by the wind and sand. These plants can live for upto 2,000 years. Spines protect the cactuslike euphorbias' fleshy arms from browsing mammals. Stone plants look so much like small rocks that grazing animals just pass them by. Semidesert with thin *scrub* (tracts of scraggly, stunted trees and shrubs) extends inland from the Namib and merges into the arid grasslands of the Kalahari Desert.

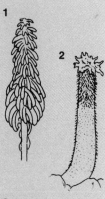

- ▢ Desert
- ▢ Semidesert

## Heath and high grassland

**Typical plants**
1 Heath species
2 King protea
3 Monarch of the veld

Short prairie grasses cover the eastern Highveld plateau of South Africa at heights of about 4,000–7,000 ft (1,200–2,100 m). Frosty winters and frequent fires help to prevent tree growth in this region. Periodic fires also helped to create the fynbos heathland of the far south. This is a mixture of brush and small trees. Scrub thrives in this region of summer drought and winter rain. Plants include low evergreen heaths (woody shrubs), the miniature-sunflowerlike monarch of the veld, herbaceous milkworts, and shrubby proteas. Proteas feature species with big, colorful flowers that produce seeds which germinate only after being scorched by fire. The western Cape area alone has more than 8,500 plant species, many of which are found nowhere else in the world. There are more than 600 species of heath, 100 proteas, and 115 milkworts. This land bursts into flower in the Cape spring of August and September.

- ▢ High grassland
- ▢ Fynbos heathland

sand dunes, great expanses consist of dry grasslands. The far south of Southern Africa is heath land with thousands of unique species – mainly shrubs and soft-stemmed flowering plants. On fertile soils people have largely replaced the natural vegetation with crops. Villagers grow food crops to supply their needs and there are also large farms and plantations, which grow crops to sell for export.

## Savanna and forest

Much of the north of Southern Africa is *savanna* (grasslands with scattered trees and shrubs). Arid savanna with thin, acacia woodland covers much of the Kalahari Desert and northern Namibia. During the summer rainy season, grasses thrive in the Kalahari. Thinly-wooded, arid savanna with small or medium sized mopane trees, which annually shed their leaves to combat drought, extends along the Limpopo River Valley. Mesic savanna covers areas of higher rainfall. These regions are patchworks of open woodland, grasslands, and dense thicket (areas of small trees and shrubs). Pockets of forest grow mainly along the Great Escarpment – a series of mountains and cliffs that separate the coastal lowlands from the interior. Tall, forest trees rim rivers and ravines in Mozambique. Tree species include ebony, ironwood, and khaya – a species with a timber like mahogany. Stinkwood, yellowwood, and candlewood trees thrive in the tall, cool coastal forests of the south.

**Typical plants**
1 Coconut palm
2 Acacia
3 Mopane

1

2

3

KALAHARI
DESERT

☐ Arid savannah
☐ Mesic savannah
■ Forest

## Madagascar

Madagascar broke away from Africa millions of years ago and has since developed many unique species. Best known of all is the traveler's-tree, with its long-stalked leaves that can store around 2 pt (0.5 l) of water. The natural vegetation of much of west and central Madagascar is deciduous forest (made up of trees that shed their leaves annually) or tracts of tall grasses interspersed with clumps of bamboo and slender trees. Temperate forest once occupied the high central plateau and a strip of tropical *rainforest*, of which only fragments now remain, stood on the coastal plain in the east. Several unique species of aloe (plants with fleshy-leaves that have spiny edges) grow on the central plateau, and coconut palms line Madagascar's sandy beaches. People have tamed much of the land: burning or cutting down trees and replacing forests with rice fields or grassland for cattle. Some natural vegetation survives, however, especially in the south which is largely too dry and hot for farming. Small, thorny shrubs and trees and members of the unique, cactuslike *Didiereacaea* family – for example, *Pachypodium lamerei* – grow in this arid region.

**Typical plants**
1 Traveler's-tree
2 *Aloe capitata*
3 *Pachypodium lamerei*

1

2

3

☐ Tropical rainforest
☐ Temperate forest
☐ Deciduous forest and grassland
☐ Semidesert and desert vegetation

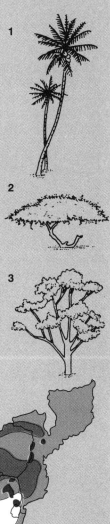

# Wildlife

Southern Africa's wide range of climate and vegetation zones supports a great diversity of wildlife. This region has nearly 340 kinds of mammals. More than half of Southern Africa's 400 or so reptile species occur only here and new kinds keep turning up. These are mainland figures and do not include those for the island "ark" of Madagascar, which has many more unique species of its own. Crops and cattle have displaced wildlife in many places, however. In Botswana, for example, thousands of gnu, or wildebeest, (cattlelike antelopes) have died

## Open countryside

Zebras and antelopes no longer roam the more fertile grasslands, which are now taken up by crops or livestock. On dry plains steinbok (small, reddish antelopes), springbok (graceful gazelles – small antelopes), and gemsbok (large antelopes with straight horns) roam. They are able to live where water is scarce. Among their enemies are lions, leopards, and packs of hunting dogs. Other dryland survivors include the insect-eating, hyenalike aardwolf; spring hare (a small, kangaroolike rodent), and the meerkat or suricate, a small, four-toed, burrowing meat-eater that lives in cooperative groups. Birds of dry, open regions include the ostrich and the pale chanting goshawk. National parks provide the last strongholds of Africa's two rhinoceros, the black and white rhino. In the desert, Peringuey's adder sidewinds over Namib sands and flowerlike feet prevent the dune cricket from sinking in.

**Typical animals**
1 Black rhinoceros
2 Springbok
3 Gemsbok
4 Hunting dog
5 Spring hare
6 Meerkat
7 Pale chanting goshawk
8 Peringuey's adder
9 Dune cricket

## Forest and woodland

Pockets of forest conceal small mammals such as the thick-tailed bush baby (a nocturnal, tree-dwelling primate with a long, bushy tail and large eyes), samango monkey (a dark monkey with long hair on its cheek and forehead), the bush pig (an African wild pig), and various tiny antelopes. The smallest antelope, the blue duiker, stands less than knee high to an adult. Larger antelopes such as the Cape eland prefer more open woodland as do small meat-eaters such as the short-legged civet cat and side-striped jackal (a wild dog). Birds of the forest include fruit-eaters such as the brightly-colored Livingstone's touraco and the tiny speckled pied barbet, which clings to trees like a woodpecker. Trees conceal a variety of snakes including the East African egg eater. Butterflies include the striking *Euphaedra neophron*.

**Typical animals**
1 Blue duiker
2 Cape eland
3 Bush pig
4 Samango monkey
5 Civet cat
6 Pied barbet
7 Livingstone's touraco
8 East African egg eater
9 *Euphaedra neophron*

since the early 1960s when new fences blocked their migration routes. Nevertheless, many large wild animals still roam areas of open countryside: the *savannas* (grasslands), deserts, and semideserts. National parks are their best hope for long-term survival, South Africa alone has seventeen. Some of these are almost overcrowded with wildlife. National parks, however, might not always be safe from a fast-multiplying human population that needs fresh land to grow food crops on.

### River, lake, and seashore

Southern Africa has a wealth of freshwater and saltwater wildlife. More than a million Cape fur seals breed around the southern coast. Seabirds include the Jackass penguin and Cape cormorant. River mouths serve as nurseries for more than 200 kinds of fishes, including the leervis (a widely-sought game fish). Inland, the freshwater Okavango Swamps teem with mammals from the hippopotamus to lechwe (swamp antelopes). Birds include skimmers, which scoop fish from the water with their flat bills. Fish include the tiny dwarf mouthbrooder, which carries its young in its mouth. Striped swamp snakes also live in the swamps. As seasonal rains flood Botswana's and Namibia's vast dry depressions called pans, billions of brine shrimps hatch, African bullfrogs emerge from mud cocoons to spawn, and ducks and waders fly in to feed.

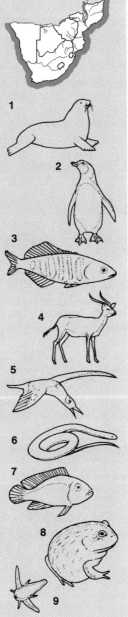

**Typical animals**
1 Cape fur seal
2 Jackass penguin
3 Leervis
4 Lechwe
5 African skimmer
6 Striped swamp snake
7 Dwarf mouthbrooder
8 African bullfrog
9 Brine shrimp

### Madagascar

Madagascar broke away from Africa millions of years ago and has since developed many unique species. The best-known of these are its lemurs (long-tailed, nocturnal primates that usually live in trees). The rare aye-aye lemur of the *rainforest* uses its long third finger and sharp teeth to extract insects from wood. Ground-dwelling ring-tailed lemurs of the southwest are the most common lemurs. Other oddities include various small, insect-eating tenrecs who are preyed on by the foxlike fossa fossa. Unique birds include the heronlike Madagascar egret and the meat-eating helmetbird. Of over 300 butterfly species, one-third are unique to Madagascar. Reptiles include the largest chameleon in the world and a day gecko: a small, brightly-colored lizard that is found nowhere else in the world.

**Typical animals**
1 Aye-aye lemur
2 Ring-tailed lemur
3 Striped tenrec
4 Fossa fossa
5 Helmetbird
6 Madagascar egret
7 Giant chameleon
8 Day gecko
9 Madagascan clubtail butterfly

© DIAGRAM

# Chronology

Roughly 27,000 years ago, Khoisan rock art is created throughout Southern Africa at around 15,000 different sites. The paintings often vividly depict hunting scenes, as shown in this example above.

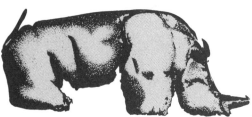

A gold rhinoceros from the ancient trading center of Mapungubwe on the Limpopo River. Unfortunately, the delicacy of the sheet metal from which such items are made means that few examples will survive until the present day.

In 1488, the Portuguese sailor Bartholomeu Dias and his crew are the first Europeans to round the Cape of Good Hope, which Dias named the Cape of Storms. King John of Portugal later renamed it the Cape of Good Hope because its discovery indicated that a sea route to India would soon be found.

## SOUTHERN AFRICAN EVENTS

Countries or locations in parentheses give the modern-day locations of the states. Dates of independence appear in a table after the chronology.

### to 999CE

| | |
|---|---|
| 25,000 BCE | Oldest examples of Khoisan rock art in Southern Africa |
| 200s CE | Bantu-speaking peoples begin to arrive in Southern Africa |
| 300s–400s | Bantu-speakers reach north and southeast of modern South Africa |
| 600s | Indonesians in Madagascar |
| 650–1300 | Large, cattle-owning, Iron-Age "Toutswe tradition" communities in existence (Botswana) |
| 900s | Bambandyanalo/Mapungubwe trading center on Limpopo River |
| 1000s | Bantu-speakers migrate from mainland to Madagascar. Major Iron-Age settlement, Leopard Kopje, built (Zimbabwe) |

### 1001–11500

| | |
|---|---|
| 1100s | Great Zimbabwe civilization develops (Zimbabwe) |
| 1100–1300 | Bambandyanalo/Mapungubwe at height of prosperity |
| 1300s–1400s | Great Zimbabwe building and trading at height. Muslim trading colonies and kingdoms established on Madagascar |
| by 1500 | Great Zimbabwe site abandoned; civilization moves north and Mutapa Empire established |
| 1500s–1700s | Successive Tsonga kingdoms, Nyaka, Tembe, and Maputo flourish (Mozambique) |

### 1501–1800

| | |
|---|---|
| 1506 | Portuguese dominate gold trade |
| 1511 | Portuguese discover the uninhabited island of Mauritius |
| 1590s | Dutch trading ships begin to stop for supplies at Cape (South Africa). Dutch occupy Mauritius |
| 1652 | Dutch East India Company sets up a supply station on Cape |
| 1657 | Some Dutch East India Company soldiers are freed to become full-time farmers (Boers) on Cape |
| 1657–1677 | Khoikhoi and Boers fight over land; Khoikhoi defeated |
| 1710 | Dutch abandon Mauritius |
| 1715 | French occupy Mauritius |

## WORLD EVENTS

**c. 3500** BCE Wheel and plow invented. Sumerians in Iraq
**510** Republic of Rome established
**c. 30** CE Jesus of Nazareth crucified
**455** Vandals sack Rome
**622** Muhammad's flight to Medina: founding of Islam
**624** T'ang dynasty unites China
**793** Viking raids begin in Europe

**1066** Normans conquer England
**c. 1150** Angkor Wat built in Cambodia
**1206** Genghis Khan begins Mongol conquest of Asia
**1346–9** "Black Death" in Europe
**1368** Ming dynasty begins in China
**1492** Columbus discovers New World (Americas)

**1519–22** Magellan's world circumnavigation. Hernan Cortés conquers Aztecs
**1526** Mughal Empire founded in India. Ottomans annex Hungary
**1619** First African slaves arrive in Jamestown, Virginia
**1620** *Mayflower* reaches New England, America

| SOUTHERN AFRICAN EVENTS | WORLD EVENTS |
|---|---|
| **1795– 1799** Unsuccessful Boer rebellions against Cape authority | **1692** Salem witch trials in America |
| **1799– 1878** A series of nine Cape-Xhosa wars between Xhosa and Boers and, later, Xhosa and British: Xhosa are eventually defeated by British | **1776–83** American War of Independence |
| **by 1797** Merina kingdom on Madagascar | **1789–99** French Revolution |

### 1801–1830

| | |
|---|---|
| **1806** British take Cape from Dutch | **1803** Louisiana Purchase |
| **1806** Cape and Mauritius become British colonies | **1804** Napoleon crowned emperor of France |
| **1806** British capture Mauritius | **1807** Britain outlaws slave trade |
| **1815** Nguni kingdoms of Ndwandwe (ruled by Zwide), Ngwane (ruled by Sobhuza I), and Mthethwa (ruled by Dingiswayo) dominate region east of Drakensberg Mts | **1815** Defeat of Napoleon at Waterloo |
| **1816** Shaka becomes Zulu leader (South Africa) | **1816–28** Chile, Venezuela, Brazil, Argentina, Peru, and Uruguay gain independence from Spain and Portugal |
| **1818– 1819** Zulu-Ndwandwe war establishes Zulu supremacy in the region | |
| **1819– 1839** *Mfecane/Difaqane* period of mass migrations and wars (South Africa) | |
| **1820** 5,000 British emigrate to Cape | **1821–30** Greek war of independence leads to freedom from Ottoman rule |
| **1820s** Mzilikazi founds Ndebele kingdom on Highveld (South Africa) | |
| **1824** Moshoeshoe founds Basuto Kingdom (Lesotho) | **1823** Monroe Doctrine in US |
| **1830s** Ngoni state of Gaza emerges (Mozambique) | |

### 1831–1850

| | |
|---|---|
| **1831** Sotho defeat invading Ndebele | **1845–51** "Potato Famine" in Ireland |
| **1836– 1848** Great Trek brings Boers into conflict with people on Highveld | **1846–8** War between US and Mexico leads to US acquisition of Texas, California, New Mexico, and most of Arizona |
| **1836** *Voortrekkers* battle with Ndebele | |
| **1837** Boers drive Ndebele from Highveld; Ndebele migrate north to reform kingdom (Zimbabwe – where they become Matabele) | |
| **1838** Zulu defeated by Boers at Battle of Blood River | **1842** Britain annexes Hong Kong from China |
| **1839** Boer republic of Natalia created | |
| **1841** Mayotte (one of the Comoros Islands) becomes a French colony | **1848** Marx and Engels publish *Communist Manifesto* |
| **1843** Natalia seized by British; colony of Natal established | |
| **1839– 1865** Reign of Mswati I over Ngwane: creation of powerful Swazi nation | |
| **1848** British annex lands on Highveld | **1849** Californian gold rush begins |

During the *Mfecane/Difaqane* (1819–39), Zulu warriors such as these form the spearhead of Shaka's attacks on neighboring peoples. The rise of the Zulu kingdom has a huge impact on the whole of Southern Africa.

A nineteenth-century Xhosa warrior. The Xhosa are the first Bantu-speaking people to come into conflict with the white settlers (the Boers and the British) from the Cape. During the 1770s, the Boers begin to encroach onto Xhosa territory and a series of Cape-Xhosa wars follow that span the next century.

© DIAGRAM

In 1905, the world's largest uncut diamond, the "Cullinan" is found in Transvaal. The "Star of Africa" stone *(left)* that is cut from it in 1908 is then incorporated into the British crown jewels.

The discovery of gold in Southern Africa in the late 1800s causes a huge gold rush and eventually leads to the establishment of colonial rule. This Krugerrand, a South African coin, contains 1 oz (28 g) of pure gold.

This banknote *(below)* is issued by the British while under seige at Mafeking (present-day Mafikeng) during the Anglo-Boer War (1899–1902). This war introduces new tactics, such as trench warfare, commando raids, and the use of concentration camps, which come to be features of many twentieth-century wars.

| SOUTHERN AFRICAN EVENTS | WORLD EVENTS |
|---|---|
| **1851–1880** | |
| 1851– Sotho-British wars I and II; British 1852 withdraw from Highveld | **1857–9** Indian Mutiny; India becomes a British |
| 1852 South African Republic (Transvaal) created by Boers | vice-royalty |
| 1854 Orange Free State (OFS) created by Boers | **1859** Darwin publishes *The Origin of Species* |
| 1855 Basuto Kingdom reaches height | |
| 1858 OFS-Sotho War I sets boundaries | **1859–61** Unification of Italy carried out |
| 1858– War between Boer republics; 1864 Transvaal unites with others | **1861–5** US Civil War |
| 1860– Venda and Sotho drive Boers out 1867 from lands north of Olifants River | **1865** US abolishes slavery |
| 1865– OFS-Sotho War II; Basuto made 1868 into British colony of Basutoland | **1867** Karl Marx publishes |
| 1867 First diamond found in Vaal Valley | *Das Kapital* |
| 1868 Gold rush in Tati Valley | **1868** Meiji |
| 1871 British annex diamond fields; De Beers and Kimberley mines grow | Restoration in Japan |
| 1876 Transvaal-Pedi War | **1869** Suez Canal opened |
| 1877 British annex Transvaal | **1871** German |
| 1879 British defeat Pedi – with help of Swazi – and Zulu | Empire proclaimed |
| 1880 De Beers Mining Co. formed | **1875** Alexander Graham Bell |
| 1880– "Gun War": Sotho rebel when 1881 British try to disarm them | invents the telephone |
| 1880– Transvaal Boers rebel against 1881 British rule; British withdraw | |
| **1881–1900** | |
| 1883 Franco-Merina War (Madagascar) | **1882** Germany, Austria, and Italy |
| 1883– Zulu Civil War after British 1884 partition Zululand | form Triple Alliance against France |
| 1883– Paul Kruger is president of 1902 Transvaal Republic | **1884** In London, UK, first underground railroad built |
| 1884– Bechuanaland, British colony, 1885 established over Tswana. Comoros made a French colony | **1885** Canadian Pacific railroad completed. Karl |
| 1884 Germans colonize South West Africa (Namibia) | Benz builds first successful |
| 1885– Zululand divided between British 1887 Zululand and Transvaal | gasoline-engined automobile |
| 1886 Gold rush on Witwatersrand; Johannesburg founded | **1886–96** Attempts to establish Irish |
| 1889 De Beers' monopoly over African diamond mining is complete | Home Rule fail in British parliament |
| 1890 British South Africa Company colonizes Southern Rhodesia | **1898** Spanish– American War |
| 1894 Swaziland made a British colony | |
| 1895 French colonize Madagascar | |

PEOPLES OF SOUTHERN AFRICA

## SOUTHERN AFRICAN EVENTS

| | |
|---|---|
| 1899–1902 | Anglo-Boer War; Boers defeated by British |

**1901–1950**

| | |
|---|---|
| 1904–1905 | Herero uprising brutally suppressed in South West Africa |
| 1910 | White-ruled Union of South Africa unites British Cape and Natal colonies and Boer republics |
| 1912 | Afrikaner-based National Party and South African Native National Congress (SANNC) formed |
| 1914–1918 | World War I, German colonies transferred to South Africa |
| 1920 | Zululand joins South Africa |
| 1923 | SANNC becomes African National Congress (ANC) |
| 1928 | Inkatha, Zulu nationalist movement, founded |
| 1939–1945 | World War II; manufacturing industries expand in South Africa |
| 1944 | ANC Youth League formed |
| 1948 | *Apartheid* begins in South Africa |

**1951–1970**

| | |
|---|---|
| 1952 | Antiapartheid Defiance Campaign in South Africa |
| 1953 | Southern and Northern Rhodesia and Nyasaland form white-ruled Central African Federation (CAF) |
| 1960 | South West Africa People's Organization (SWAPO) founded |
| 1962 | Formation of Frente de Libertação de Moçambique (Frelimo). Zimbabwe African People's Union (ZAPU) formed (S. Rhodesia) |
| 1963 | Zimbabwe African National Union (ZANU) formed. CAF dissolves |
| 1964 | Nelson Mandela imprisoned |
| 1965 | Illegal white-minority regime established in Northern Rhodesia, which becomes Rhodesia |
| 1966 | SWAPO rebels begin operations against South African forces. Basutoland renamed Lesotho. Bechuanaland renamed Botswana |
| 1967–1975 | Period of guerrilla warfare against white Rhodesians. |
| 1969 | United Nations declares South Africa's occupation of South West Africa illegal |

## WORLD EVENTS

**1891** Trans-Siberian railroad begun
**1904–5** Russo-Japanese War
**1914–18** World War I (WWI)
**1917** US enters WWI. Second Russian Revolution; socialism adopted
**1929** Wall Street crash in US
**1930s** Worldwide depression
**1939–1945** World War II (WWII)
**1941** US in WWII
**1946–1947** Cold War begins
**1949** Communists take China
**1950–3** Korean War
**1952** First contraceptive pill ("The Pill") made
**1955** Warsaw Pact is signed by communist East Europe
**1957** War between North and South Vietnam begins
**1959** Cuban revolution led by Fidel Castro
**1962** Cuban missile crisis
**1963** US President J. F. Kennedy is assassinated
**1965–73** US involvement in Vietnam War
**1967** Six-Day War between Israel and Arab nations
**1968** Assassination

The old flag of South Africa features the flags of Britain and the Boer republics, which united with the British colonies in 1910 to form the Union of South Africa. In 1934, South Africa approves independence from Britain and leaves the Commonwealth in 1961, but this flag is kept until 1994.

The insignia of the South West Africa People's Organization (SWAPO). This organization leads the resistance against South Africa's illegal occupation of Namibia.

These white women are being taught to shoot during the outbreak of guerrilla war in Rhodesia. Ian Smith's illegal Unilateral Declaration of Independence (UDI) in 1965 sets up a white-minortiy government and is strongly opposed by the majority of the population, many of whom take up arms against the regime. These women, however, are prepared to fight to protect themselves and Smith's regime.

© DIAGRAM

*Apartheid*, in effect from 1948 to 1991 in South Africa, uses force and official classifications of "race" and ethnicity to oppress the majority of the population. Separate houses of representation are created for "Colored" and Indian voters in 1983, but in a ratio that keeps the balance of power in the hands of the whites. Many people choose not to vote, as the author of this graffiti in Johannesburg demands.

These supporters of Prime Minister Robert Mugabe are celebrating the independence of Zimbabwe (formerly Rhodesia) from white-minority rule in 1980.

| SOUTHERN AFRICAN EVENTS | WORLD EVENTS |
|---|---|
| **1971–1990** | |
| **1972** Military take over in Madagascar | of Dr Martin Luther |
| **1973** Swaziland bans political parties and king assumes absolute power | King in Tennessee **1969** Neil |
| **1975** Inkatha reconvened. Frelimo forms government in newly-independent Mozambique and Resistência Nacional Mocambicana (Renamo) rebels begin civil war | Armstrong is first man on the Moon **1973** Oil Crisis after Arabs ban oil sales to US **1974** "Watergate" |
| **1976** Rioting in South Africa dealt with harshly by government. ZAPU and ZANU merge to form Patriotic Front (PF) resistance movement | scandal in US. **1975** Communists reunite Vietnam |
| **1978** Mercenaries oust Comoros' president. South Africa bombs SWAPO refugee camp | **1978–9** Iranian revolution **1979** Civil wars in |
| **1979** Lesotho bans opposition parties | Nicaragua and El Salvador |
| **1980** End of white-minority rule in Rhodesia; African government renames Rhodesia Zimbabwe | **1979–88** USSR in Afghanistan **1980–8** Iran-Iraq |
| **1986** South Africa blockades Lesotho; military coup in Lesotho. South Africa declares state of emergency after escalating troubles in *townships* | War; US backs Iraq **1982–5** Israel invades Lebanon **1989** Revolution in Romania |
| **1990** In South Africa, Nelson Mandela is released; ANC ends armed struggle; talks with government begin; state of emergency ended | **1990** Gulf War begins. East and West Germany are reunited |
| **1991–1996** | |
| **1991** One-party system abandoned in Zimbabwe. Official end of apartheid. Military coup in Lesotho | Breakup of USSR and Yugoslavia Gulf War ends. |
| **1992** ANC drops out of talks with government after massacre by security forces at Boipatong. Mozambique's civil war ends | Cold War ends. Riots in LA. War in former Yugoslavia spreads to Bosnia |
| **1993** Elections end dictatorship in Madagascar. Lesotho returns to civilian rule after elections | Israeli-PLO peace. World Trade Center bomb kills six in US |
| **1994** ANC wins first nonracial elections in South Africa; Nelson Mandela is first black president. South Africa returns Walvis Bay to Namibia. Attempted military coup in Lesotho led by King Letsie III | US intervention in Haiti. Cease-fire announced by IRA. Civil war erupts in Rwanda. Military coup in Gambia |

| SOUTHERN AFRICAN EVENTS | | WORLD EVENTS |
|---|---|---|
| **1995** | Letsie III abdicates and Moshoeshoe II, his father, becomes Lesotho's king. Former apartheid leaders in court for hit-squad murders. Military coup in Comoros. All Africa Games are held in Zimbabwe | Israeli prime minister assassinated. Peace agreement reached in former Yugoslavia |
| **1996** | Floods in KwaZulu/Natal kill 100. South Africa wins African Nations Football Cup. Marathon runner Josia Thugwane becomes first black South African to win an Olympic gold medal. Mozambique joins the Community of Portuguese-speaking Countries. Moshoeshoe II killed in a car crash. Opening of Truth and Reconciliation Commission in South Africa, which attempts to heal divisions of apartheid era | IRA ends cease-fire. TWA airliner explodes off Long Island, NY, killing 230 passengers and crew. Outbreaks of Arab-Israeli violence increase in Israel and Palestine. Troubles in Rwanda spread to Burundi |

## COLONIAL OCCUPATION AND INDEPENDENCE

| Country | Independence | Occupied* | Colonial power |
|---|---|---|---|
| Botswana as (Bechuanaland) | Sept 30, 1966 | 1885 | Britain |
| Comoros | July 6, 1975 | 1843 | France |
| Lesotho (as Basutoland) | Oct 4, 1966 | 1868 | Britain |
| Madagascar | June 26, 1960 | 1895 | France |
| Mauritius | March 12, 1968 | 1715 | France 1715–1810; Britain 1810–1968 |
| Mozambique | June 25, 1975 | 1505 | Portugal |
| Namibia (as South West Africa) | March 21, 1990 | 1884 | Germany 1884–1919; occupied by South Africa 1915–90 |
| Swaziland | Sept 6, 1968 | 1894 | Britain (administered by the Boer's South African Republic 1894–1902) |
| Zimbabwe (as Southern Rhodesia then Rhodesia) | 18 April, 1980 | 1890 | Britain |

*The years given for the beginning of colonial occupation of the modern-day nation states are those by which a significant area of coastal and hinterland territory had been effectively occupied by a colonial power.

In 1994, former prime minister of KwaZulu homeland and leader of Inkatha, Chief Mangosthutu Gatsha Buthelezi becomes Minister for Home Affairs in South Africa's first democratically elected government.

This silk screen poster is made in 1986. Between 1948 and 1991 opposition to *apartheid* takes many forms. In particular, much of South African art highlights the inequalities and injustices of apartheid.

© DIAGRAM

# Pictorial history

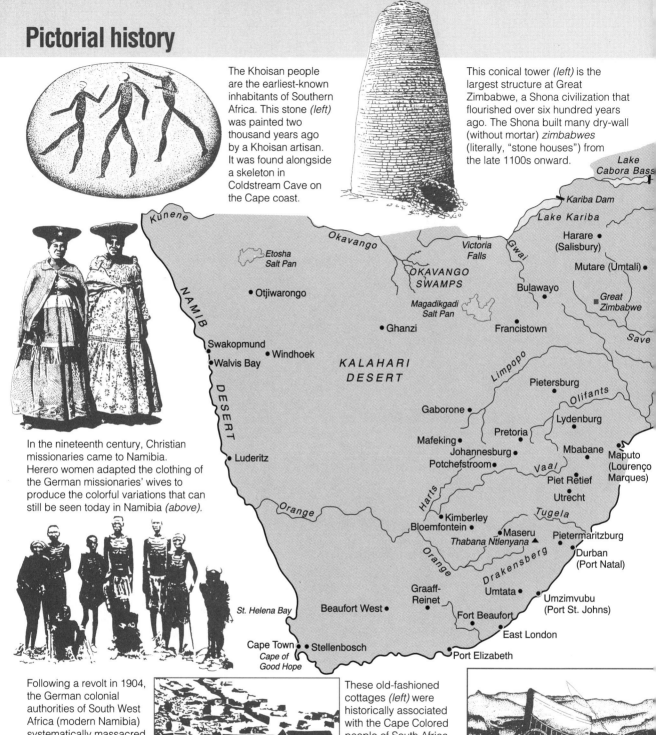

The Khoisan people are the earliest-known inhabitants of Southern Africa. This stone *(left)* was painted two thousand years ago by a Khoisan artisan. It was found alongside a skeleton in Coldstream Cave on the Cape coast.

This conical tower *(left)* is the largest structure at Great Zimbabwe, a Shona civilization that flourished over six hundred years ago. The Shona built many dry-wall (without mortar) *zimbabwes* (literally, "stone houses") from the late 1100s onward.

In the nineteenth century, Christian missionaries came to Namibia. Herero women adapted the clothing of the German missionaries' wives to produce the colorful variations that can still be seen today in Namibia *(above)*.

Following a revolt in 1904, the German colonial authorities of South West Africa (modern Namibia) systematically massacred the Herero people, more than three-quarters died as a result – they were either killed outright or died from starvation as these victims above did.

These old-fashioned cottages *(left)* were historically associated with the Cape Colored people of South Africa. Today, these people of mixed African, European, and Asian descent live, fully integrated, in the modern towns and cities of the Cape region.

Lake Cabora Bass
Kariba Dam
Lake Kariba
Harare •
(Salisbury)
Mutare (Umtali) •
Great
Zimbabwe
Save
Bulawayo
Francistown
Victoria
Falls
Gwai
OKAVANGO
SWAMPS
Okavango
Magadikgadi
Salt Pan
Kúnene
Etosha
Salt Pan
Otjiwarongo •
Ghanzi •
KALAHARI
DESERT
Limpopo
Pietersburg •
Olifants
Lydenburg •
Gaborone •
Pretoria •
Mafeking •
Johannesburg •
Mbabane •
Maputo
(Lourenço
Marques)
Potchefstroom •
Vaal
Piet Retief •
Utrecht •
Tugela
Kimberley •
Bloemfontein •
Maseru •
Pietermaritzburg
Thabana Ntlenyana ▲
Durban
(Port Natal)
Drakensberg
Umtata •
Umzimvubu
(Port St. Johns)
East London
Graaff-
Reinet •
Beaufort West •
Fort Beaufort •
Port Elizabeth
Cape Town •• Stellenbosch
Cape of
Good Hope
St. Helena Bay
Orange
Harts
Orange
Swakopmund •
• Windhoek
• Walvis Bay
NAMIB
DESERT
• Luderitz

22

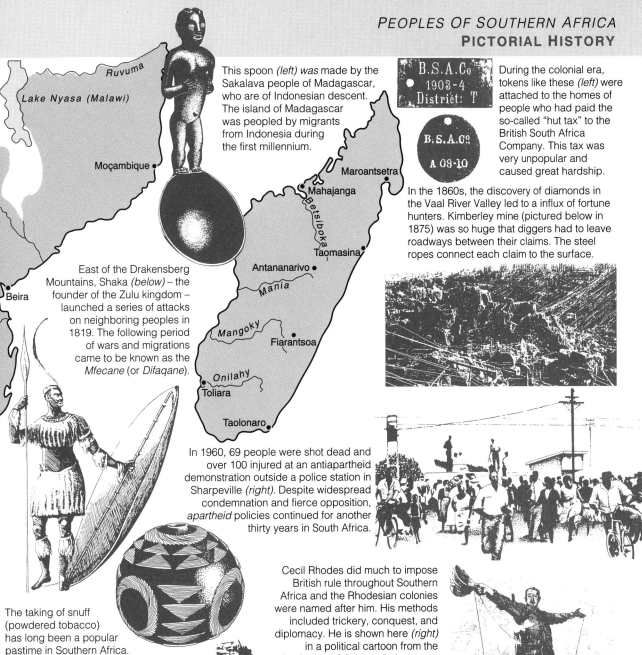

This spoon (left) was made by the Sakalava people of Madagascar, who are of Indonesian descent. The island of Madagascar was peopled by migrants from Indonesia during the first millennium.

During the colonial era, tokens like these (left) were attached to the homes of people who had paid the so-called "hut tax" to the British South Africa Company. This tax was very unpopular and caused great hardship.

B.S.A.Co
1903-4
District: T

B.S.A.Co
A 09-10

In the 1860s, the discovery of diamonds in the Vaal River Valley led to a influx of fortune hunters. Kimberley mine (pictured below in 1875) was so huge that diggers had to leave roadways between their claims. The steel ropes connect each claim to the surface.

East of the Drakensberg Mountains, Shaka (below) – the founder of the Zulu kingdom – launched a series of attacks on neighboring peoples in 1819. The following period of wars and migrations came to be known as the Mfecane (or Difaqane).

In 1960, 69 people were shot dead and over 100 injured at an antiapartheid demonstration outside a police station in Sharpeville (right). Despite widespread condemnation and fierce opposition, apartheid policies continued for another thirty years in South Africa.

The taking of snuff (powdered tobacco) has long been a popular pastime in Southern Africa. This snuff container (right) was made by a Zulu artisan.

Cecil Rhodes did much to impose British rule throughout Southern Africa and the Rhodesian colonies were named after him. His methods included trickery, conquest, and diplomacy. He is shown here (right) in a political cartoon from the beginning of the twentieth century that satirizes his, failed, ambition to conquer all of Africa from "the Cape to Cairo."

A series of mass northeastward migrations of Boers (Afrikaners) from 1836 to 1848 came to be called the Great Trek and its participants Voortrekkers (left).

On the right are Boer (Afrikaner) guerrillas pictured during the Anglo-Boer War (1899–1902). The Boers fought using commando raids and guerrilla tactics to try to stay independent from Britain.

© DIAGRAM

23

# Distribution of peoples

**1 Ovambo**
The Ovambo live on the plains that straddle the border between Angola and Namibia. They form the largest single ethnic group in Namibia. The Ovambo language is also called Ovambo. The vast majority of Ovambo are Christians.

**2 Herero**
Most Herero live in Namibia but a few are also in Botswana, where many settled after a brutal German massacre at the beginning of the twentieth century. The Herero language is also called Herero. The vast majority of Herero are Christians and the women are recognizable for their "leg o' mutton" dresses, which were adapted from nineteenth-century German missionary fashions.

**3 Khoisan**
The Khoisan live mainly in the arid regions of Botswana and Namibia and a few have recently moved to South Africa. The Khoisan are the earliest-known inhabitants of Southern Africa and have lived in the region for thousands of years. The Khoisan speak various Khoisan languages and mostly follow their own religions.

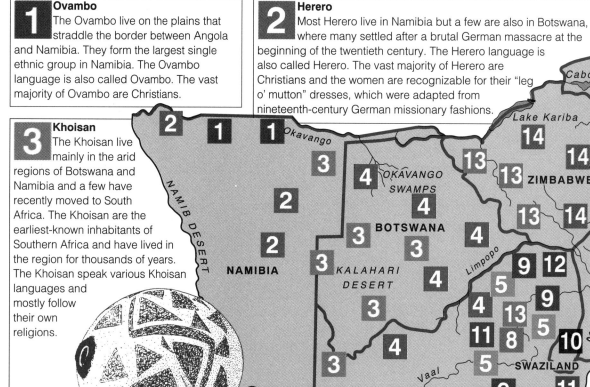

**4 Tswana**
The Tswana (or Batswana) are the main ethnic group in Botswana and from a significant minority in South Africa. They are closely related to the Sotho people. The Tswana language is Setswana. Most Tswana people are Christians, yet the Tswana religion is still widely followed.

**5 Afrikaners**
The Afrikaners live mainly in South Africa though significant numbers can be found in Namibia. The Afrikaners are descended from Dutch farmers (Boers), who settled on the Cape of Good Hope in the seventeenth century, and local African populations. The Afrikaner language is called Afrikaans – a descendant of Dutch. The vast majority of Afrikaners are Christians.

**6 Cape Coloreds and Cape Malays**
The Cape Coloreds and the Cape Malays live mainly around the Cape region of South Africa. They are descended from European, Asian, and African ancestors. The major difference between the two groups is religion: most Cape Coloreds are Christian and the vast majority of Cape Malays are Muslim. Both groups speak Afrikaans. Some reject the classification of Cape Coloreds as a separate ethnic group believing it to be a legacy of *apartheid* (South Africa's racist doctrine of "separate development").

**7 Indian South Africans**
Indians first came to South Africa as contracted laborers; they were followed by businessmen and traders. Today, they form a small but economically influential minority in the republic. Indian South Africans speak a variety of Indian languages. The vast majority are either Muslim or Hindu.

Lake Nyasa (Malawi)

Kuvuma

**MOZAMBIQUE**

mbezi

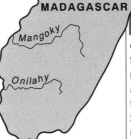

Betsiboka

Mania

**MADAGASCAR**

Mangoky

Onilahy

**15 Madagascan peoples**

Madagascans are descended from Asian, African, and Arab immigrants to the island. Indonesians were the first to arrive – in the first millennium. There are eighteen principal ethnic groups on the island. Many kingdoms flourished on Madagascar but the most powerful was the nineteenth-century Merina kingdom. Many dialects of Malagasy are spoken on Madagascar and many religions followed, though over a quarter of the population are Christian.

**14 Shona**

The Shona are the largest ethnic group in Zimbabwe. They have a long history of centralized civilization and were responsible for the building of Great Zimbabwe, the ruins of which mystified historians for years – they could not accept that an indigenous African society created them. The language of the Shona is also called Shona. Although the majority of Shona are Christians, the Shona religion is still strong.

**10 Swazi**

The Swazi form the majority of the population of the kingdom of Swaziland and a few live in neigboring areas of South Africa. The Swazi kingdom was founded in the nineteenth century. The Swazi language is called Swazi. While over half the Swazi are Christians, the Swazi religion is still widely practiced.

**11 Zulu**

The Zulu live mostly in the South African province of KwaZulu/Natal, previously the KwaZulu *homeland*. They are one of the largest and best known of South Africa's ethnic groups. The Zulu language is also called Zulu. In the nineteenth century, the Zulu kingdom dominated the region of northeastern South Africa. Christianity and the Zulu religion coexist in many Zulu communities.

**13 Ndebele and Matabele**

The Ndebele and the Matabele are sometimes both referred to as Ndebele people. The Ndebele live in South Africa and the Matabele in Zimbabwe. The Matable are an Ndebele group who migrated north from present-day South Africa to modern Zimbabawe in the previous century. Ndebele women are famous for their beadwork and mural art. Both groups speak Ndebele and the vast majority are Christians.

**12 Venda**

The Venda live in the far northeast of South Africa. Their initiation rites for girls, which involve the famous python dance, attract much attention. The Venda language is Luvenda and the majority of Venda are Christians.

**8 Xhosa**

The Xhosa live in the southeastern regions of South Africa. During the eighteenth and nineteenth centuries, they fought a long campaign of resistance to British and Boer expansion. The Xhosa language is also called Xhosa and the vast majority are Christians, though aspects of the Xhosa religion still remain.

**9 Sotho**

The Sotho form the majority of the population of the Lesotho Kingdom and a few also live in neighboring regions of South Africa. The Lesotho Kingdom was established in the early nineteenth century. The Sotho languages are called Northern Sotho and Sesotho. The majority of Sotho are Christians, yet many still follow the Sotho religion.

© DIAGRAM

# Introduction

T he peoples of Southern Africa reflect a wide variety of lifestyles and cultures. This book describes a selected sample of these cultures, where possible detailing contemporary changes and the impacts they have had on people's lives.

## The peopling of Southern Africa

The original inhabitants of Southern Africa were ancestors of the contemporary Khoisan people. Over many hundreds of years, these people retreated or were absorbed as others migrated into the area and, today, relatively few direct descendants remain. The majority of Southern Africans are descendants of Bantu-speaking peoples who originated from present-day eastern Nigeria. At first, they spread through the equatorial *rainforest* belt and then eastward and southward into East and Southern Africa. Bantu people occupied the southern grasslands of present-day Zambia and Zimbabwe by the beginning of the Common Era. The first groups crossed the Limpopo River into present-day South Africa in the early centuries of the first millennium. Until recently, some scholars disputed this early arrival of Bantu people in Southern Africa. Largely motivated by political reasons, they wished to prove that European settlers arrived in South Africa around the same time as the Bantu people did and, therefore, had equally legitimate claims to the land. Recent archeological evidence has proved, however, that Bantu-speaking peoples had been established in South Africa for at least thirteen centuries before Europeans arrived in the mid-1600s. By the fifteenth century at least, two major cultural and linguistic Bantu groupings had emerged: the Nguni (in the southeast of South Africa) and the Sotho-Tswana complex (on the Highveld). The Zulu, Ndebele, Matabele, Swazi, and Xhosa are all Nguni in origin. Many East Africans are descended from Nguni refugees who fled the violence of the *Mfecane/Difaqane* in the mid-1800s – they are known as Ngoni peoples. The Shona and Venda, while still Bantu peoples, share a separate origin to the north of the Limpopo. Another major grouping is the Tsonga of Mozambique, from whom the Nguni may be descended.

Meanwhile, Madagascar was peopled in successive waves of migration. The earliest migrants were people of Malayo-Polynesian origin but over the years they were joined by immigrants from Africa, Asia, Arabia, and Europe.

## Historical overview

Before the arrival of Bantu speakers, the Khoisan lived mainly by hunting and gathering. The Bantu peoples brought with them ironworking techniques, *pastoralism* (livestock keeping), and hoe-cultivation. These developments enabled the evolution and growth of new economies. Wealthy kingdoms developed based on farming, cattle-keeping, and trade in gold and ivory. The early Shona kingdoms (such as Great Zimbabwe) of present-day Zimbabwe, for instance, largely based their prosperity on long-distance trade, farming, and raising cattle.

By the mid-seventeenth century – as Dutch people began settling on the Cape coast – nations existed over most of Southern Africa. The Dutch settlers were joined by the British in the nineteenth century and rivalry between the two European groups lead to the migration of many Boers (Afrikaner farmers) into areas controlled by the African kingdoms. In the mid-nineteenth century, many Boers embarked upon the Great Trek – a mass northeastward migration away from the Cape. This coincided with a period of great turmoil and conflict in the region to which they were headed. Known as the Mfecane (or Difaqane), this period of migrations and wars was the crucible from which many new states emerged: the Zulu, Swazi, Sotho, Ndebele, and Matabele kingdoms, for example. The opportunistic Boers benefited as they were able to establish their own republics in the recently-devastated region.

After the discovery of gold and diamonds in the region, the British attempted to colonize much of present-day South Africa. Despite great resistance, by 1910 all of Southern Africa was under European (British, German, French, or Portuguese) or Boer rule. The colonial era saw the institution of white-minority rule in Namibia (as South West Africa), Zimbabwe (as Southern Rhodesia and then Rhodesia), and South Africa. The final vestiges of white-minority rule in Southern Africa have only recently been overturned by South Africa's 1994 multiracial elections.

## Geography

Southern Africa comprises the Southern Plateau; the Great Escarpment, which rims the Southern Plateau; the southern tip of the Great Rift Valley; and coastal lowlands. The Great Rift Valley is a depression that extends from the Jordan River valley in southwest Asia across most of East Africa and as far south as Mozambique. In the past, it acted as a corridor facilitating the peopling of Africa. The land of Southern Africa can be divided into three main categories: desert and semidesert; *savanna*; and mountainous regions. Important geographical features include the swampy Okavango Delta, the major rivers (Vaal, Orange, and Limpopo, for example), the Drakensberg Mountains, and the Cape of Good Hope, which projects into the Atlantic Ocean.

Most of the *savanna* lands (flat, rolling grasslands and open woodlands) lie within the Southern Plateau as do the desert and semidesert regions. Semidesert regions occur largely on the edge of the two main deserts – the Kalahari (actually a semidesert) and the Namib. They have sparse vegetation and periodic *droughts* (periods of inadequate rainfall). *Desertification* (land becoming desertlike) has become a problem in some arid regions as overuse combined with inadequate rainfall tires the soil out. Mountainous regions have their own distinct high-altitude environments.

The nation of Madagascar lies in the Indian Ocean and comprises a large island (Madagascar) and several smaller satellite islands. The island of Madagascar has a central mountainous area surrounded by a region of coastal lowlands. The southern end is mostly desert but the north has more fertile soils. Madagascar has Southern Africa's only tropical rainforests and boasts many unique plants and animals.

## People today

The population figures provided for each ethnic group are estimates from between 1980 and 1996. The peoples selected for inclusion tend to be distributed across more than one country. It is difficult, therefore, to use national censuses (which vary in frequency and amount from nation to nation) to gather up-to-date information about a people's numbers. Statistics have been taken instead from a variety of sociological and anthropological sources; they have been included only to indicate the size and relative importance of a group.

The vast majority of Southern Africans are Black Africans. A considerable minority, however, are not: for example, there are Afrikaners, English-speaking people, Indian, Malay, and Khoisan people. Through migration, conquest, and intermingling, the people of Southern Africa have diversified over the years into many different ethnic groups. It is difficult and often inappropriate, therefore, to classify people according to physical appearance or race. Also, national boundaries were colonial inventions and do not necessarily relate to ethnic groups or historical African states. Ethnic groups are more a matter of cultural, linguistic, historical, religious, and perceived similarities than race or nationality. South Africa's use of ethnicity to divide and rule the majority of the population has left many Southern Africans sensitive to the issue. For instance, the word Bantu is a valid linguistic classification but its misuse by the old South African government has left it tainted with derogatory implications.

Hundreds of languages are spoken in Southern Africa. Many are particular to certain ethnic groups, while others are widely spoken due to historical factors. Shona, for instance, is used widely as it was an important trading language. English, Portuguese, and French have been used in Southern Africa since the colonial era. The result of this diversity is that many people can speak more than one language.

There are also many religions in Southern Africa. The bulk of these are particular to certain ethnic groups. The most widespread religion in Southern Africa, however, is Christianity – often practiced in conjunction with an African religion. Southern Africa was introduced to Christianity by European missionaries in the nineteenth century while the Afrikaners brought their own Christian Church (Dutch Reformed) with them from Holland. Christianity only really flourished in the region, however, after the emergence of the many independent Churches with predominantly African congregations and clergy.

## Lifestyles

The population of Southern Africa is mostly rural. This fact hides a huge variety of lifestyles, however – South Africans, in particular, have a very urbanized society. Many people are farmers; others are traders, scholars, weavers, doctors, artists – there are as many occupations as you would expect to find in any contemporary society. It is difficult, therefore, to describe the typical lifestyle of any specific group of people. Many Southern Africans are also employed away from their home as migrant laborers on farms or down mines. The larger farms tend to be owned by whites. In most countries *underemployment* has lead to the growth of thriving informal sectors in which people create their own job opportunities. As would be expected, *apartheid* (South Africa's racist doctrine of "separate development") has had a huge impact on the lifestyle of many South Africans, restricting them to low-paid, menial, and unskilled professions. During apartheid, many South Africans were forced to live in *homelands* based on their ethnic group. Although these have since been reincorporated into South Africa, they have been included on some of the peoples locator maps as they still provide a rough guide to the areas in which a group is most concentrated.

## Recent changes

The most significant change in Southern Africa has been the demise of apartheid, which had a great impact not only on the lives of South African citizens but on the lives of most Southern Africans. Within South Africa itself, apartheid has left behind a legacy of inequality, poverty, and conflict that will take many years to reverse. Furthermore, in order to protect the status quo in South Africa, neighboring states were deliberately destabilized and impoverished by the apartheid regime.

# Afrikaners

O ver three million Afrikaners live in South Africa, representing about sixty percent of the country's so-called "white" population and less than ten percent of all South Africans. In addition, about 70,000 Afrikaners live in Namibia, comprising roughly five percent of the country's population. Elsewhere in Africa, many of the large-scale farmers in Kenya and Zimbabwe were Afrikaners, but recently their numbers and economic importance have declined. Today, because of *drought* (inadequate rainfall) and pressure on farming land, small but increasing numbers of Afrikaner farmers are emigrating and taking their skills and capital to other parts of Africa as part of government relocation schemes, especially to Congo, Zambia, Mozambique, and Tanzania.

## History

In 1652, the Dutch East India Company founded a garrison and supply station on the Cape of Good Hope for ships sailing between Holland and Asia. In 1688, 156 French Protestant refugees (Huguenots) arrived in the Cape. The Company encouraged the establishment of farms around Cape Town to supply the garrison and passing ships. The African-born children of the settlers

### Afrikaners timeline

| | |
|---|---|
| 1652 | Dutch garrison established on the Cape of Good Hope |
| 1657 | Some Dutch soldiers become farmers (Boers) on Cape. Conflict with local Khoikhoi people over land begins |
| 1795– 1799 | Unsuccessful Boer rebellions against Cape authority |
| 1799– 1878 | Series of nine Cape-Xhosa wars; Xhosa lands annexed |
| 1806 | British annex Cape Colony |
| 1807 | British ban slave trade |
| 1819– 1839 | *Mfecane/Difaqane*: period of mass migrations and wars |
| 1833 | British abolish slavery |
| 1836– 1848 | Great Trek brings Boers into conflict with people inland |
| 1838 | Boers defeat Zulu at Battle of Blood River |
| 1839 | Boer republic, Natalia, created |
| 1843 | British take Natalia |
| 1852 | South African Republic (Transvaal) created by Boers |
| 1854 | Orange Free State (OFS) created by Boers |
| 1899– 1902 | Boers defeated by British in Anglo-Boer War |
| 1910 | Boers and British form white-ruled Union of South Africa |
| 1912 | Afrikaner-based National Party (NP) formed |
| 1934 | South Africa approves independence from Britain |
| 1948 | *Apartheid* officially introduced |
| 1961 | South Africa becomes a republic |
| 1991 | Apartheid legislation repealed |
| 1994 | First nonracial elections held |
| 1996 | New constitution adopted |

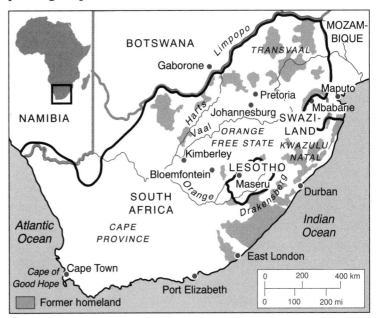

### Trekboers

A group of Afrikaner farmers (Boers) accompanied by their Khoikhoi herdsmen and herds of sheep and cattle. During the 1700s, such *trekboers* (migrant farmers) led the colonization of areas inland as they moved farther away from the Cape in search of new pastures. As the land of one farm was exhausted they moved on to another, and as sons reached adulthood they established their own farms. In this way, the Boers claimed huge areas of land for themselves.

became known as "Afrikaners," the first recorded use of the term being in 1707. Until the early nineteenth century, "Afrikaner" carried few racial connotations, being applied to people of mixed European, African, and Malay origin as well as those of solely European ancestry. Later, being an Afrikaner came to imply being "white," with people of mixed descent classified as "colored." Many Afrikaners are descendants of interracial unions, though few admit so.

Over the years, tension developed between the Dutch authorities and the Boers (the Dutch for "farmer" and the historical name of the Afrikaners), many of whom moved inland to escape what they felt was oppressive rule. In the interior, away from Company influence, the Afrikaner as a distinct group emerged. In 1806, the British took permanent control of Cape Town. Unwilling to live under British rule, many more Afrikaners journeyed north and east into the African interior in the Great Trek of the 1830s, which became a legendary event in Afrikaner history. These migrants, the *Voortrekkers,* met fierce resistance from Bantu-speaking inhabitants such as the Zulu and Xhosa. Their victories in battle are still celebrated as proof of divine intervention and of the righteousness of their mission.

### Piet Retief

An Afrikaner of French Huguenot descent and the commander of a militia, Piet Retief published a manifesto in 1837 setting out the reasons behind the Great Trek (1836–48). His complaints included:

*We despair of saving the colony from the turbulent and dishonest conduct of vagrants...the severe losses which we have been forced to sustain by the emancipation of our slaves...the continual plunder which we have endured from the Caffres* [the Xhosa] *and other colored classes....*

© DIAGRAM

## The Great Trek and the first Boer republics (1836–54)

Large-scale treks begun in 1836 came to be called the Great Trek and its participants *Voortrekkers*. Afrikaner farmers wishing to be independent, especially from British rules and regulations, organized large family groups to travel inland away from the Cape. For the years that they were on the move, the trekkers led a *nomadic* existence, stopping for a few days wherever grass and water were found. Progress was slow and only a few miles were covered each day. Some groups ventured east over the Drakensberg Mountains where they encountered the Zulu. Despite their victory over the Zulu at Blood River in 1838 and the establishment of the Natalia republic in 1839, the Afrikaners trekked back over the mountains after Natalia was annexed by the British in 1843. West of the Drakensberg, on the Highveld north of the Orange River, several independent Boer republics had been established. Annexed by the British in 1848, they were recognized as independent from 1852 and came to form the Orange Free State and the South African Republic (which became Transvaal).

The 1838 victory at Blood River, when 500 Boers defeated 10,000 Zulu, is especially remembered and is claimed to be the result of a pact with God – though this pact was never mentioned until after the event. The Voortrekkers established independent republics that became Transvaal, Orange Free State, and Natalia. The British annexed these republics but later returned them to independence (except Natalia, which became Natal).

In 1886, gold was discovered in Transvaal, leading to the arrival of thousands of fortune seekers. When the British sent troops into Transvaal they met fierce resistance, resulting in the Anglo-Boer War (1899–1902). Even today, bitterness toward the British remains, with memories of the loss of some 7,000 men in battle and of the 18,000 to 28,000 women and children who died in British concentration camps.

**APARTHEID** In 1948, the National Party came to power in South Africa – mainly thanks to the support of poor and rural Afrikaners. *Apartheid* (the racist doctrine of "separate development") was the government's main

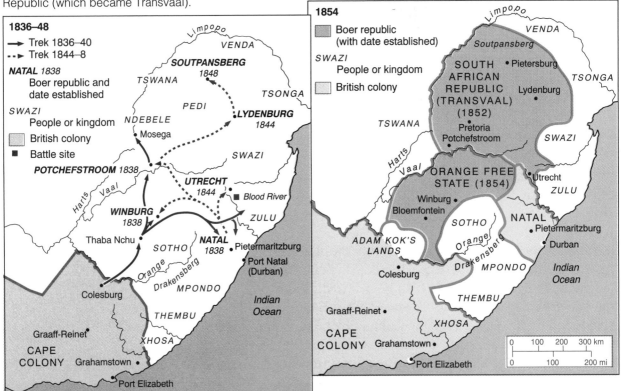

political platform, with many of its ideals inspired by Nazi Germany. Most Afrikaners supported apartheid, but some were fierce critics and joined nonracial churches, the illegal Communist Party, or the African National Congress. Branded as traitors, some were forced into exile, imprisoned, or put under house arrest. **RECENT EVENTS** In 1991, a reformist National Party government ended all apartheid laws, and in 1994, South Africa's first nonracial elections were held, bringing to an end Afrikaner-dominated rule. Unlike many South Africans of British origin, Afrikaners have not been leaving the country in significant numbers. Afrikaners consider themselves to be Africans and, in the immediate future, they are likely to remain an economically-privileged minority within South Africa.

**The Anglo-Boer War (1899–1902)**
These Afrikaner women are being taken to a British concentration camp. After the discovery of gold and diamonds in the region, the British set about conquering most of present-day South Africa including the Boer republics. In an attempt to wipe out Boer resistance, the British adopted a "scorched earth" policy – Afrikaner women and children were forcibly moved to concentration camps and their farms were destroyed in order to deny the Boer guerrillas access to food and supplies. Housed in wooden huts or tents with inadequate food and water supplies, many camp internees died from disease or starvation.

## Language

Afrikaners speak Afrikaans, a language closely related to Dutch. The early European settlers' need to communicate with their slaves encouraged the grammatical restructuring of Dutch and the incorporation of words from Malay and African languages. The Afrikaans vocabulary further developed with the necessity of finding new words to express observations and sentiments relating to Africa, as well

© DIAGRAM

**Boer guerrillas**
Facing a much better equipped enemy during the Anglo-Boer War (1899–1902), the Boers adopted guerrilla tactics. At first, they were successful in resisting the British. After the establishment of concentration camps by the British and the destruction of their farms, however, the guerrillas found it hard to continue their successes.

**Voortrekker Monument**
Opened in 1949 by Prime Minister Malan, the Voortrekker Monument near Pretoria commemorates the Great Trek of the mid-nineteenth century. It has become an important symbol for the Afrikaner people.

as incorporating French, German, and English influences. Afrikaans played an important role in the growth of Afrikaner nationalism, especially in terms of resistance to British rule and English influence, and the language remains central to Afrikaner identity. For 250 years, Dutch was the official language of the Afrikaners' church and schools. Official recognition of Afrikaans was hampered as it had no tradition as a written language, but in 1925 Afrikaans replaced Dutch as South Africa's official language alongside English. Today, most Afrikaners speak English as well as Afrikaans, with many rural Afrikaners also speaking other African languages. In 1995, the status of Afrikaans was reduced to one of eleven official South African languages, to the dismay of many Afrikaners.

## Ways of life
In 1946, only about forty percent of Afrikaners lived in urban areas, but fifty years later the figure was over eighty percent. While fifty years ago poverty, especially in rural areas, was still widespread, today the majority of Afrikaners have a lifestyle that is comparable to that of middle-class or wealthy North Americans.

Under apartheid, the Afrikaners' economically privileged position was protected by law, with most of South Africa's best land and jobs reserved for them and their white compatriots. Business was largely controlled by English-speaking South Africans. Following the National Party victory in 1948, however, Afrikaners became a significant business presence. When apartheid was no longer sustainable, it was working-class and junior-level white-collar Afrikaners who felt most threatened. The jobs of many such individuals were dependent on their race rather than on their skills and, as such, they were in the forefront of the stubborn resistance to political change.

## Social structure
Afrikaner social structure differs little from that of North Americans or Europeans. Most Afrikaners can trace their ancestry to a relatively small number of

Dutch or French Protestant settlers, but this ancestry is more important for social standing than for wealth.

## Culture and religion

**RELIGION** Most Afrikaners are members of the Calvinist Dutch Reformed Church, which bases its teachings on the Old Testament. Early Afrikaners saw themselves as Israelites – God's chosen people – with the British representing the Pharaoh, and the grasslands of the African interior the Promised Land. The Dutch Reformed Church sanctioned apartheid by arguing that it was God's will. Today, all but the most conservative churches have, at least officially, rejected apartheid.

**LITERATURE** Although prior to 1900 Afrikaans was not a written language (the Afrikaans translation of the Bible only appeared in 1933), Afrikaners have a rich literary heritage. Especially significant has been poetry, an ideal means to experiment with a rapidly developing language. Since the 1960s, poets and novelists such as Breyten Breytenbach and André Brink have shocked and angered the Afrikaner establishment because of the sexual content and antiapartheid themes of their work, much of which was banned from publication.

**MUSIC** Due to their religious backgrounds, most early Afrikaner households owned a harmonium, or pedal organ, which was used at evening prayer meetings. This instrument, along with the concertina and guitar, formed the basis of *Boeremusiek* – light, danceable country music, using arrangements popular with Afrikaners. As it is easier to transport, the accordion has replaced the harmonium to a great extent. Many of the melodies originated in Europe, but the lyrics have been adapted to suit local interests. Boeremusiek can be heard at large-scale music festivals or at private *braaivleis* parties (barbecues).

**SPORT** Competitive sport is extremely popular among Afrikaners, who are most associated with rugby. Banned from international competitions until recently, the South African rugby team (which is still dominated by white players) reentered world sport with a resounding victory in the 1995 rugby World Cup.

© DIAGRAM

**Paul Kruger**
President of the Transvaal Republic (1883–1902), Kruger had no formal education but established himself as a leader by fighting heroically in a commando unit against both other Africans and the British. He was a strong and forceful champion of Afrikaner interests and tried to free his republic from British domination.

**Eugene Terre' Blanche**
As leader of the Afrikaner Resistance Movement, or Afrikaner Weerstandsbeweging (AWB), Terre' Blanche represents the fears of mostly poorer, rural Afrikaners who felt they would lose most from the end of *apartheid*. His extreme right-wing party formed in 1973 and adopted many Nazi symbols. The AWB is only one of many militant white right-wing groups.

35

# The rise and fall of apartheid

Apartheid *(the Afrikaans word for "apartness")* *was the name given to South Africa's policy of racial segregation, discrimination, and white domination that was in force from 1948 to 1991.*

## The roots of apartheid

*By the time apartheid was officially introduced, racist policies had been practiced for over three hundred years in South Africa. The Dutch who settled on the Cape in the seventeenth century soon established semislave relationships with the local Khoikhoi population – whose way of life became dependent on Afrikaner (the name the Dutch settlers later adopted) employment. The Boers (the Dutch word for farmers) then began to import slaves from other parts of Africa and elsewhere to provide cheap labor for building and farming work.*

*In the nineteenth century, Britain took Cape Colony from the Dutch. In 1807, they outlawed slave trading – though slaves could still be kept legally – and, in 1820, about 4,000 Britons settled in the Cape. Unable to purchase slaves legally and with no free labor available, the new settlers set about wresting the Afrikaners' slaves from them by decreeing that nobody, of whatever color, could be forced into service. This was followed by the abolition of slavery throughout the British Empire in 1833. Combined with other changes, this threatened to destroy the Afrikaners' lifestyle, and, in 1836, they began to trek to the interior of Africa where they planned to live unhampered by British bureaucrats. The Afrikaner republics that were set up en route of this Great Trek had as the bases of their constitutions the right of Afrikaner self-determination and the "right" to rule the "natives."*

*After the discovery of huge diamond and gold reserves, the British set about conquering the whole of present-day South Africa. The Afrikaners were defeated by the British during the Anglo-Boer War*

**J. B. M. Hertzog** *(right)*
A Boer general in the Anglo-Boer War (1899–1902), Barry Hertzog was prime minister from 1924 to 1939. Hertzog created the Ministry of Native – later, Bantu – Affairs in 1910 and founded the Afrikaner-based National Party in 1912, two institutions that were central to *apartheid*.

**Dr Daniel François Malan** *(left)*
Malan was prime minister from 1948 to 1954. He was a fierce Afrikaner nationalist and his cabinet was the first to consist entirely of Afrikaners and to use only Afrikaans. Malan promoted Afrikaner interests above those of anyone else.

*(1899–1902). A liberal backlash in Britain over the cruel measures used to win the war, however, set the agenda for Anglo-Boer conciliation. In 1910, the British colonies and the Afrikaner republics (most of which had been given their independence back in 1907) united to form the white-ruled Union of South Africa. Louis Botha, an Afrikaner, was the first prime minister.*

*Over the years, the Afrikaners – who were mainly farmers or, later, part of the underclass of urban workers – came to resent the British, who dominated the lucrative mining industry, skilled professions, the military, and the civil service. Indeed, the strident Afrikaner nationalist sentiment that emerged had developed largely as a result of British imperialism and domination. This nationalism was turned on the black population in force after the National Party (NP) – formed in 1912 to further Afrikaner interests – came to power in 1924. This does not mean, however, that English-speaking South Africans were not in collusion with the Afrikaners in the creation of apartheid.*

## The 1948 election

*The NP merged, in 1934, with another party to form the United Party, which addressed the interests of both English-speakers and Afrikaners. The remnants of the NP were resurrected by the Broederbond (an influential, secret nationalist Afrikaner society) and other Afrikaner extremists led by Dr Daniel François Malan. This "purified" National Party came to power in 1948 promising to create apartheid. Malan promised to send all black people to reserves, run a white-only economy, and "to save civilization from black hordes" — a task he claimed to be ordained by God. This message appealed to many white industrial workers who feared competition from the black majority for their jobs. Apartheid was also welcomed by the mine owners and white farmers as it allowed them to maintain the profitable — for them — status quo. In order to provide themselves with cheap labor, mine owners had long been employing black workers and installing them in cramped, single-sex barracks.*

## Apartheid in practice

*Apartheid was different from the racial segregation practiced historically in South Africa because it was enshrined in, and enforced by, the law. Under*

**The architect of apartheid**
Under Malan, *apartheid* was largely a vote-winning slogan. It was Dr Hendrik Verwoerd – Minister of Native Affairs from 1950 to 1958 and prime minister from 1958 to 1966 – who actually introduced the policies needed to make apartheid a reality. Verwoerd tried to justify apartheid by describing it as "separate development of the races." He was assassinated in 1966.

*J. B. M. Hertzog the Ministry of Native – later, Bantu – Affairs (created in 1910) began drafting some of the laws and policies that formed the bones of apartheid. Although many racist policies were in place before 1948, after this date they were extended and enforced to a greater extent.*

**DISENFRANCHISEMENT** *At the heart of apartheid was the denial of voting rights to all but the white population. Like other policies, disenfranchisement had a long history. The first Afrikaner republics of the 1800s had only allowed Afrikaner men to vote. Also, the British passed a law to deny black people the right to vote outside the Cape. Within the Cape, few could meet the strict educational and financial requirements needed to qualify. Indian and "Colored" voters were given separate houses of representation in 1983, but in a ratio that ensured continued white domination. In protest, many did not exercise their right to vote.*

**RELOCATION** *Relocation policies aimed to limit the number of black people staying overnight in "white" towns and to segregate people within urban areas. After the 1913 Native Land Act, black South Africans were allowed to buy or rent land only in "native reserves." Over sixty percent of the*

**Segregation of amenities**
After the Defiance Campaign of civil disobedience in 1952, the government introduced the Separate Amenities Act. Separate facilities had to be provided for different races and this included public benches, beaches, and even stairways. The bill also stated that the facilities did not have to be of an equal standard.

NET NIE BLANKES.
NON EUROPEANS ONLY.

*population was restricted to living in only 7.3 percent of the land (later increased to 13 percent). Denied access to land, black South Africans had to work for the white population, who needed their labor on farms, in towns, and down the mines. The*

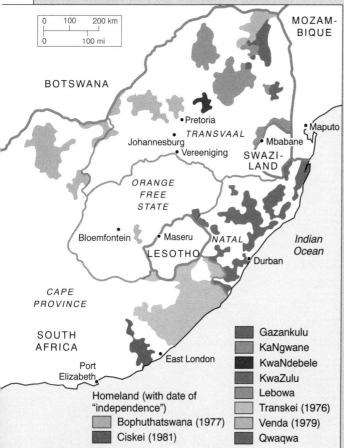

0   100   200 km

0        100 mi

MOZAM-BIQUE

BOTSWANA

• Pretoria

*TRANSVAAL*

Johannesburg •

• Vereeniging

• Mbabane

• Maputo

SWAZI-LAND

*ORANGE FREE STATE*

Bloemfontein •

• Maseru

*NATAL*

*Indian Ocean*

LESOTHO

• Durban

*CAPE PROVINCE*

SOUTH AFRICA

Port Elizabeth

• East London

Gazankulu

KaNgwane

KwaNdebele

KwaZulu

Lebowa

Transkei (1976)

Venda (1979)

Qwaqwa

Homeland (with date of "independence")

Bophuthatswana (1977)

Ciskei (1981)

### Homelands

At first self-governing – as long as the Minister of Bantu Affairs approved – many homelands were given their "independence" after 1970. This independence was not recognized anywhere but inside South Africa as it was simply an excuse for the government not to concern itself with the provision of facilities. More importantly, the inhabitants of homelands could be denied any rights in the rest of South Africa as they were now "foreign" nationals. Homelands were wholly dependent on external areas for work: industries were encouraged to set up on the edge of homelands but not inside. Most homeland leaders – with the exception of Chief Buthelezi, Prime Minister of KwaZulu – were supporters of apartheid.

*1948 Group Areas Act created separate residential and business areas for each officially-designated race into which people could be forcibly moved.*

**HOMELANDS** *By the 1960s, it was obvious that the reserves were unviable; they were overpopulated and under-resourced, and starvation was widespread. Nevertheless, in 1959 the 260 reserves were organized into several homelands or Bantustans. Despite segregationist policies, sixty percent of the black population lived in "white" areas in 1948. Between 1960 and 1983, however, over three million people were evicted to live in the homelands.*

**COLOR BARS** *Color bars prevented the majority of South Africans from doing many things, such as working as skilled professionals. Unofficial color bars had long been in existence in the mining industry, for example. White workers filled supervisory and skilled positions while black workers were left to do the lower-paid manual jobs. When the mines tried to promote black workers to supervisory positions in 1922 – simply to save money on wages – strikes and demonstrations by white miners nearly caused a civil war. Two years later the NP came to power with the support of the white-only trade unions and immediately legalized color bars.*

**BANTU EDUCATION** *In 1955, the Bantu Education Act was passed. After this date, many students were denied the right to a high-standard academic education. Instead, a poor-quality education was provided as approved by the Department of Native (Bantu) Affairs. Schools that refused to conform were closed down and reluctant teachers sacked.*

**POPULATION REGISTRATION ACT** *Under this act, every South African was required to register and be classified by "race," which would then be stamped in his or her identity pass. This would then be used to determine, for example, where people could live, what job they could do, and who they could marry.*

**PASS LAWS** *The first pass law – the Hottentot Code – was introduced by the British to the Cape Colony*

**Pass laws**
During *apartheid*, pass laws were used to enforce racial segregation. Every black person had to carry a pass – with an employer's stamp if they were in a "white" town. Police could stop people at any time to check their passes.

occupied by South Africa (as South West Africa) until 1990 and a form of apartheid was introduced. South Africa easily pressured Lesotho and Swaziland, which are economically reliant on the goodwill of South Africa, into supportive roles. Border blockades were often used to force Lesotho's policies into line.

## Opposition to apartheid

Opposition to apartheid was widespread, involved people of all colors, and took many forms. The first

in 1809. It required that all Khoikhoi have a fixed place of abode and a pass with an employer's stamp if they needed to travel. This law forced the Khoikhoi to work for the Afrikaners in order to get a pass. Although repealed a few years later – in order to create a mobile supply of workers for the British settlers – it was the first of many similar laws. Pass laws gave the authorities power to restrict people's access to towns, send others back to homelands, and ensured the supply of labor to the white population.

### Front-line states

Wealthy and heavily armed, South Africa was able to dominate neighboring countries – the front-line states in the fight against apartheid – in order to protect its own policies. Intimidation, sabotage, military action, and subversion were all used to destabilize the regimes that South Africa found threatening and prop up those that supported it – the illegal white-minority regime in Rhodesia (present-day Zimbabwe), for example. Using the excuse of trying to eliminate its enemies' guerrilla bases, South Africa invaded many front-line states. Angola was invaded, bombed, and – along with Mozambique – subjected to a prolonged civil war due, in part, to South Africa's funding of rebel groups. Other East and Central African countries suffered from these problems through the influx of refugees from war zones. Namibia was illegally

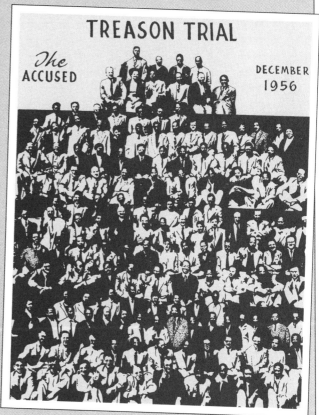

**Treason Trial**
The 1956 "Treason Trial" of 156 people involved in the 1952 Defiance Campaign – including Nelson Mandela – lasted until 1961. All charges were eventually dismissed as the defendants' nonviolent principles did not substantiate the government's claim that they had incited violence. The trial attracted worldwide attention, which enabled the International Defense and Aid Fund to be established to fund antiapartheid activities.

**Sharpeville massacre**
In 1960, a demonstration organized by the newly-formed Pan-Africanist Congress (PAC) outside a police station in Sharpeville was fired on by the police. Sixty-nine people were killed – most were shot in the back – and over one hundred were injured.

*organized resistance was led by Mohandas Karamchand Gandhi, an Indian lawyer, who came to Natal in 1893 and stayed until 1914. Using nonviolent methods and recourse to the law, Gandhi was an inspiration to later movements. The South African Native National Congress – it became the African National Congress (ANC) in 1923 – was formed in 1912. Its first leaders – John L. Dube, president, and Sol Plaatje, secretary – attempted to effect changes by appealing to Britain and challenging unjust laws in court. The government's stubborn refusal to reform, however, led to the*

**Steve Biko**
Medical student Steve Biko was the leading thinker of the *Black Consciousness* movement, which emerged in the 1970s. He believed that oppression had caused many to feel that they really were inferior to whites and argued that pride in being black should be cultivated instead. Biko was arrested in 1977 and killed while in police custody.

*development of more militant methods. The ANC really became a mass movement only in 1944 with the founding of the ANC Youth League by Anton Lembede. His colleagues included Nelson Mandela, Walter Sisulu, and Oliver Tambo.*

*One of the first examples of successful mass political mobilization was the Defiance Campaign of 1952. With Indian and other groups and using trained volunteers, the ANC orchestrated local defiances of unjust laws all over the country. The campaign was called off after outbreaks of violence occurred. Reprisals by the government were often severe. Police powers were increased to deal with the growing unrest caused by apartheid. Torture and informers were widely used and many died in police custody. More "humane" methods included the banning and restraining orders put on political activists in order to halt their activities.*

*In 1961, as president of the ANC, Tambo left South Africa to open overseas offices of the ANC. From Lusaka, Zambia, he organized guerrilla forays into South Africa and raised funds. In the same year, Mandela formed the Umkonto we Sizwe (Spear of the Nation) movement, which was to perform sabotage on economically important facilities – but to avoid harming people – in order to pressure the government into talks. The initial result was that Mandela and Sisulu, among others, were*

imprisoned for life in 1964.

Huge uprisings led by the schoolchildren of Soweto (the southwestern townships of Johannesburg) followed the announcement, in 1976, that Bantu education would be in Afrikaans. Protests escalated and strikes brought Johannesburg to a standstill. Police response was harsh, and by the end of the year over five hundred people, including many children, had been killed.

Most opposition leaders were committed to nonviolent methods (Desmond Tutu won the Nobel Peace Prize for his nonviolent campaigning) but this was sometimes ignored by others. Apartheid policies of segregation, not only by race but also by ethnic group, inevitably led to outbreaks of what came to be called "black-on-black" violence – though many incidents were no doubt incited by government agents. Although Chief Buthelezi's Zulu Inkatha movement (originally formed in 1928 and reconvened in 1975) and Mandela's Umkonto were mutually supportive, their members often clashed.

### The fall of apartheid

Deaf to moral arguments, economic reasons for the government to end apartheid brought matters to a crisis point. Even before the 1948 elections, serious drawbacks to segregationist policies had become obvious. The government soon discovered that labor provided by the excluded majority was vital for the fastest-growing sector of the economy: manufacturing industries. This labor force also needed to be well-educated and mobile enough to be efficient – impossible within apartheid. Employers, especially in the construction sector, often had to ignore color bars just to fill vacancies. After the Sharpeville massacre in 1960 and the 1970s Soweto uprisings, foreign investment halted, capital flowed out of the country, house prices and the share market slumped, and businesses collapsed. In many ways, apartheid did not make sound economic sense. Pressure at home and from abroad was also making the system increasingly unworkable. As increasing numbers of African and Asian countries joined the United Nations, calls for sanctions against South Africa grew. Antiapartheid movements had been arguing for sanctions for years and, in 1985, many international banks paid heed. Loans were not renewed and the promise of future ones withdrawn. In 1990, Mandela was released from prison and, in 1991, all apartheid legislation was repealed. Finally, in 1994, the first nonracial elections were held in South Africa and Mandela was elected president. The inequalities that apartheid created over many years will not disappear overnight though.

**1994 elections**
South Africa's first nonracial elections were held in 1994 and Nelson Mandela, as leader of the ANC, was elected president.

# Cape Coloreds and Cape Malays

Cape Coloreds are people of mixed European, African, and Asian origin from the Cape region of South Africa. Most of the 3.5 million people of mixed race in South Africa and the around 150,000 people of mixed race elsewhere in Southern Africa are of Cape Colored origin. Many South Africans reject the label "Cape Colored," believing the term to be a legacy of *apartheid* (the racist doctrine of "separate development"). Others feel that the existence of Cape Colored people with a rich cultural and racial heritage is a reality.

Cape Malays are of mixed Malay, Indian, Sinhalese, Arab, Madagascan, and Chinese origin. Most of the 90,000 or so Cape Malays live in or around Cape Town.

## History

In 1652, the Dutch East India Company founded Cape Town as a garrison and supply station for ships sailing between Holland and Asia. Relationships between Dutch settlers and Khoikhoi women were common and many children resulted. During the seventeenth and eighteenth centuries, slaves were introduced into the region from Asia and from other parts of Africa. Interracial marriages and casual sexual encounters were common and the Cape Colored and Cape Malay peoples gradually emerged from this mix. By the late nineteenth century, the Cape Coloreds formed a distinct group.

## Language

Both Cape Coloreds and Cape Malays speak Afrikaans.

### Cape Colored and Cape Malay timeline

| | |
|---|---|
| 25,000 BCE | Oldest examples of Khoisan rock art in Southern Africa |
| c. 400s | Some Khoisan begin to keep livestock: Khoikhoi emerge |
| 1652 CE | Dutch garrison established on the Cape of Good Hope. Dutch and Khoikhoi mix |
| 1600s–1800s | African and Asian slaves brought to Cape; Cape Colored population emerges |
| 1806 | British annex Cape Colony |
| 1807 | British ban slave trade |
| 1819–1839 | *Mfecane/Difaqane*: period of mass migrations and wars |
| 1833 | British abolish slavery |
| 1910 | Boers and British form white-ruled Union of South Africa |
| 1927 | First Immorality Act bans extramarital intercourse between "Europeans" and "natives" |
| 1934 | South Africa approves independence from Britain |
| 1948 | *Apartheid* officially introduced |
| 1949 | Second Immorality Act bans interracial marriages |
| 1950 | Population Registration Act |
| 1951 | Colored voting rights removed |
| 1961 | South Africa becomes a republic; leaves Commonwealth |
| 1983 | Separate House of Representation given to Cape Colored voters |
| 1984–1989 | Many people refuse to vote in elections for new house |
| 1991 | Apartheid legislation repealed |
| 1994 | First nonracial elections held |
| 1996 | New constitution adopted |

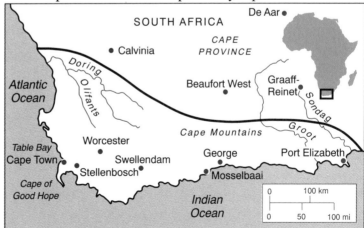

## Ways of life

The introduction of apartheid in 1948 led to restrictions on South Africa's majority population, including the Cape Coloreds and Cape Malays. Marriage between members of the different "racial" groups was made illegal – extramarital sexual relations were already illegal – and segregation prevented people of different racial origins from living in the same districts. The 1950 Population Registration Act enforced definitions of "race" – based on physical appearance as well as general acceptance and "repute." A person's race then dictated much of what they could do. Classifications were absurd; many families were divided; and many people were evicted from their homes or lost their jobs. Although apartheid has ended, the inequalities it produced remain. Cape Coloreds are found in all occupations, though the legacy of apartheid means many are unskilled or semiskilled workers. The rich farmlands of Western Cape are largely dependent on the labor of poorly paid Cape Coloreds. Cape Malays are renowned as artisans, small traders, and fishermen.

**Cape Colored architecture**
An historic Cape Colored rural village in Cape Province. Today, few families still live in traditional whitewashed stone houses such as these; most Cape Coloreds now live in the towns and cities.

## Social structure

**POLITICAL STRUCTURE** In 1951, the Cape Coloreds' limited voting rights (men only, and subject to property and income qualifications) were removed. In 1983, in an attempt to divide apartheid's opponents, a new constitution was introduced giving people officially classified as "Colored" limited parliamentary representation. The overwhelming majority of these voters boycotted the 1984 and 1989 elections. In 1991, the government repealed all apartheid laws and, in 1994, South Africa's first nonracial elections were held.

**Cape Malays at prayer**
Most Cape Malays are Muslim, their religion being the prime factor that distinguishes them from the Cape Colored population. As required by Islam, Cape Malays typically dress in what they consider to be a "modest" manner, the severity of interpretation a matter of personal choice. Women generally wear long dresses or skirts, long sleeves and a head scarf. Men dress as other urban South Africans though many wear a *fez* (a brimless felt hat) or a small, white prayer cap.

## Culture and religion

The culture of the Cape Coloreds is in most respects no different from that of Afrikaners of similar social and economic backgrounds.
**RELIGION** Like Afrikaners, most Cape Coloreds are members of Dutch Reformed churches, though separate wings were created for each racial group. The vast majority of Cape Malays are Muslim.

© DIAGRAM

# Herero

**Herero timeline**

**c. 1500s** Herero arrive in Namibia
**1825–** Herero establish supremacy
**1870** over local Khoisan people
**1884** Germany colonizes Namibia as South West Africa; Christianity introduced to region
**1884–** British colonize Botswana
**1885** as Bechuanaland
**1904–** Herero uprising against
**1905** German rule led by Samuel Maherero; many Herero are massacred and others flee to Bechuanaland
**1910** White-minority ruled Union of South Africa formed
**1914–** Herero encouraged to revolt
**1918** during WWII by South Africa
**1915** South West Africa occupied by South Africa: Herero restricted to inadequate "native reserves"
**1920s** Herero nationalism develops
**1948** Form of *apartheid* introduced
**1960** South West Africa People's Organization (SWAPO) formed
**1966** Botswana independent. Conflict between SWAPO and South African troops begins
**1969** South Africa's occupation of South West Africa declared illegal by United Nations
**1989** Apartheid-style legislation repealed in South West Africa
**1990** South West Africa gains independence as Namibia
**1996** Herero demand compensation from Germany for 1904–5 massacre from Chancellor Kohl on his visit to Namibia

In precolonial times, the Herero lived throughout the plateau area of central Namibia, but today they are widely dispersed, concentrated in small areas on the plateau they once dominated. While the overwhelming majority of Herero live in Namibia, there are also smaller numbers in northwest Botswana. The Herero were once one of Namibia's most numerous peoples, but today they number approximately 75,000, about seven percent of the country's population.

## History

The Herero and Ovambo share a common early history of migration, probably originating in the region around the great lakes of East and Central Africa. Like the Ovambo, the Herero probably arrived in Namibia in the fifteenth or sixteenth century from what is now Zambia. By the late seventeenth century, the Herero had reached the arid Kaokoveld Plateau, bringing with them their herds of long-horned cattle. By the eighteenth century, they had moved on south to the superior grazing lands of central Namibia. Unlike the Ovambo, the Herero virtually abandoned agriculture, concentrating almost exclusively on raising cattle.

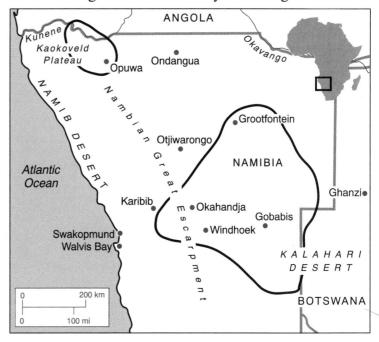

**COLONIALISM** In the nineteenth century, European traders, explorers, and missionaries entered Herero territory. In 1884, Germany claimed Namibia (as South West Africa), including the Herero's territory, as a colony. German settlers gradually seized Herero grazing land and property, even confiscating Herero cattle for "trespassing" on their newly acquired lands.

In 1904, the Herero staged a revolt. Their leader, Samuel Maherero, decreed that only German soldiers and male settlers should be attacked – women, missionaries, English, and Afrikaners should be spared. The Herero warriors were no match for German weaponry, however, and Maherero and his followers fled into the Kalahari Desert. The German commander then ordered his forces to exterminate the Herero. In the six months before Germany ordered a halt to the genocide, the Herero were reduced by bullets, poison, thirst, and starvation from a population estimated at 75,000 to 90,000 to less than 20,000. The Herero survivors dispersed, many trekking north and east into desert and semidesert regions of Botswana (then the British colony of Bechuanaland).

**Herero fashions**
In the nineteenth century, women converts to Christianity adopted the fashions of the wives of the German missionaries: long dresses with "leg o' mutton sleeves." Even today, Herero women wear this distinctive type of dress. Unlike the dour missionary clothing, however, materials used for Herero dresses are often patterned and very colorful. They are usually worn with a turbanlike headdress.

**Victims of the Herero massacre**
After the 1904–5 uprising, German colonists ruthlessly oppressed the Herero people. Many, such as these, became victims of famine or dehydration after they were driven into desert areas by the Germans.

© DIAGRAM

45

**Herero home**
This home has been built in the classic round Herero style. The Herero make these houses from either brick or a mud and dung mixture, but with the arrival of bricks, many modern houses are now square. Aluminum siding is often used as a roof or, if the owner prefers or cannot afford modern materials, grass is made into a thatched roof.

**Milk bottle**
This antique milk bottle was made by a Herero artisan from a *calabash* and strips of leather.

**APARTHEID** The Herero hoped that South Africa's occupation of Namibia following Germany's World War I defeat would lead to positive change, but their position remained largely unaltered. Cattle ownership was again allowed but land rights were not restored. The South Africans introduced a form of *apartheid* (the racist doctrine of "separate development") that controlled the Herero's places of residence and work. Despite their relatively small numbers, the Herero played an extremely important role in the Namibian struggle for independence from South Africa, contributing several key leaders to SWAPO (South West Africa People's Organization). SWAPO was the country's resistance movement during the struggle for independence and is now its main political party.

## Language
The Herero language is called Herero (or Ojitherero); many Herero also speak other Namibian languages.

## Ways of life
The 1904–5 massacre had a huge impact on the Herero, greatly altering their ways of life. Those who remained in Namibia were placed in inadequate "native reserves" and their land and cattle distributed to German settlers for whom they worked as virtual slaves. Herero refugees arrived in Botswana without cattle and the sacred objects of their ancestors, and survived by hiring themselves out as hands to local, mainly Tswana, cattle herders. Only in the late 1920s did a resurgence of ethnic identity among the Herero in Namibia and Botswana commence, as a result of increases in prosperity and cattle ownership and the rebuilding of family networks. Until independence in 1990, the Herero in South African-controlled Namibia remained restricted to reserves (later, a *homeland*) or were employed as cattle hands on white-owned farms or as servants or laborers in the towns.
**CATTLE** Herero life has long been dominated by cattle raising. A man's herd is a measure of his social standing and individuals might own thousands

of head of cattle. Most rural labor is devoted to cattle raising and during the frequent *droughts* huge wells are dug to provide water for the herds. Men are responsible for herding; women are responsible for milking. Historically, cattle would rarely be eaten unless the animal had died by accident or naturally, but today the Herero raise cattle on a commercial basis for slaughter.

**SETTLEMENTS** The Herero live in extended family *compounds* called *ozonganda.* An ozonganda consists of one or more buildings used for sleeping and storage; a large yard for cooking, eating, and washing; and enclosures for goats and cattle. The extended family living in an ozonganda is headed by a senior male and includes his wife or wives, their children, and wives of their sons and their children. Other relatives including brothers and, especially, unmarried sisters, may also live in the ozonganda. Several ozonganda share the cost and labor of creating a well.

## Social structure

Family ancestry is extremely important for the Herero and individuals have a deep knowledge of their family history that stretches back many generations. Each Herero is a member of an *oruzo* (a line of ancestors traced through male relatives) and a *banda* (a line of ancestors traced through female relatives). These groups determine social status and inheritance rights.

## Culture and religion

**RELIGION** Most Namibian Herero are Christians. The Herero living in Botswana, however, have not adopted Christianity to any great degree. Meanwhile, their own religion, which was based on the view that cattle were bequeathed to the Herero by their ancestors, has largely died out as cattle are now viewed in more practical and less sacred terms. This has lead to the development of a primarily secular society among the Botswana Herero. The Ovahimba – a small Herero subgroup living on the isolated Kaokoveld Plateau – are considered to retain Herero culture in its most pure form.

### Ovahimba

Although the Ovahimba are a subgroup of the Herero, they are different in many ways. For example, Ovahimba clothing is very different as the women have not adopted the missionary-inspired fashions of the Herero. Instead, they are more likely to wear hide or cloth skirts with a bustlelike effect. The Ovahimba are mostly cattle herders and live on the Kaokoveld Plateau. Most practice *seminomadic pastoralism* but are increasingly finding it less necessary to migrate as water distribution facilities improve in Namibia. The home shown below, made from a wooden frame coated with mud and cow dung, is ideal for a nomadic existence. As the Ovahimba become more settled, however, more-permanent houses are being built.

© DIAGRAM

# Indian South Africans

There are around one million Indian South Africans, roughly three percent of South Africa's population. Eighty percent of these live in the province of KwaZulu/Natal (especially in and around Durban) with the remainder concentrated in the Johannesburg-Pretoria area. Indian South Africans are completely integrated into national life, unlike in East Africa where Asians' allegiances have often been viewed with suspicion.

## History

Indian laborers first came South Africa in 1860 to work on British Natal's sugar plantations, and by 1911, when recruitment was suspended, 152,000 Indians had arrived. Indians were also contracted to work on the railroads, in mines, and on tea plantations, often enduring slavelike conditions. Contracts were for five years, followed by an additional two years. After a further five years as a "free" worker, laborers were given the choice of a free passage to India or of remaining in South Africa with a small land grant. Most of the immigrants were men, but one-third were women – to the objection of many white settlers who argued

### Indian South Africans timeline

| | |
|---|---|
| 1652 | Dutch garrison established on the Cape of Good Hope |
| 1806 | British annex Cape Colony |
| 1843 | British annex Natal (present-day KwaZulu/Natal) |
| 1860 | First indentured (contract) laborers arrive from south Asia |
| 1893 | Mohandas K. Gandhi arrives in South Africa from India |
| 1910 | Boers and British form white-ruled Union of South Africa |
| 1911 | Recruitment of indentured laborers suspended |
| 1914 | Gandhi leaves South Africa |
| 1934 | South Africa approves independence from Britain |
| 1946 | Asiatic Land Tenure Act |
| 1948 | *Apartheid* officially introduced |
| 1949 | Rioting South Africans attack Indian businesses |
| 1950 | Population Registration Act restricts people to certain jobs and areas according to their officially-designated "race" |
| 1952 | Indian and other antiapartheid movements organize the nonviolent Defiance Campaign |
| 1961 | South Africa accepts Indians as legitimate citizens |
| 1983 | Separate House of Representation established for Indian voters |
| 1984–1989 | Many people refuse to vote in elections for new house |
| 1991 | End of all apartheid legislation |
| 1994 | First nonracial elections held |
| 1996 | New constitution adopted |

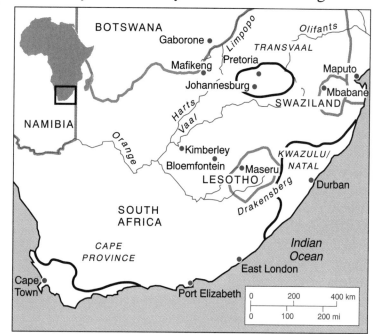

that the presence of women would encourage the creation of a stable Indian community.

Most Indians arrived in South Africa on contracts, but about ten percent went there at their own expense, most of them traders from Gujarat in western India. These often-wealthy immigrants – known as "Passengers" – formed an elite group that campaigned vigorously for political and civil rights, but their economic strength often undermined the few advances ex-indentured (contracted) laborers were making.

In 1893, a young Indian lawyer, Mohandas Karamchand Gandhi, arrived in South Africa to work in Transvaal. It was in South Africa that Gandhi – the future leader of the Indian independence movement – developed and first practiced his philosophy of nonviolent resistance and civil disobedience. Within a few years, Gandhi was regarded as an important leader of Indian South Africans, though he essentially represented the interests of "Passengers."

In 1946, just as Indians were gaining political and economic strength in South Africa, the Asiatic Land Tenure Act was introduced, restricting where they could live and trade. The 1948 electoral victory of the Afrikaner-dominated National Party led to even more restrictions on Indians. Indians – whether born in South Africa or not – were officially regarded as immigrants, "repatriation" was official policy, and Indians' limited parliamentary representation ceased. The following year, rioting by Zulus directed at Indian businesses resulted in 142 deaths, but led to an agreement between Indian and other civil rights movements – the African National Congress and the Transvaal and Natal Indian congresses – to coordinate their resistance to *apartheid* (the racist doctrine of "separate development").

**RECENT EVENTS** In 1961, the South African government officially accepted Indians as a permanent part of the country's population. In 1983, in an attempt to divide apartheid's opponents, a new constitution was introduced giving "Colored" people and Indians limited parliamentary representation. In the following year's

**Mohandas Karamchand Gandhi**
An Indian lawyer, Gandhi came to South Africa at the end of the nineteenth century and stayed until 1914. By using peaceful means of resistance – such as boycotts and civil disobedience – Gandhi highlighted the often ridiculous and illogical nature of *apartheid* laws. His tactics were adopted by many later civil rights movements. Gandhi returned to India in 1914 and led that country's campaign for independence.

© DIAGRAM

elections, however, only eighteen percent of Indians voted and the 1989 elections were also boycotted. The abolition of apartheid laws in 1991 led to all adult South Africans being given the right to vote, regardless of race. In 1994, South Africa celebrated its first nonracial elections.

## Language

Two-thirds of Indian immigrants to South Africa came from the Tamil- and Telugu-speaking areas of south and east India, while the remainder spoke Hindi, Gujarati, or Urdu. Today, English is the main language of Indian South Africans, though many also speak an Indian language, Zulu, or Afrikaans.

## Ways of Life

By the end of the nineteenth century, Indians in South Africa were no longer mainly laborers. Indians had become virtually the sole producers of fruit and vegetables for Natal's rapidly expanding cities; they were also important as artisans and retailers, and many were employed as domestic servants.

Today, less than four percent of Indians are involved in agriculture, mostly as owners of small or medium-sized sugar or market-garden farms. The overwhelming majority of Indian South Africans live in urban areas where they work as artisans, in low-level clerical occupations, in manufacturing industries, or they run their own small businesses. From the late nineteenth century, Indians have been represented in professions such as law, medicine, and education.

**EDUCATION** Under apartheid, entry to virtually all educational facilities was determined by "race," with separate schools and universities for each officially-designated race. Educational facilities for Indians were not as poor as those for black South Africans, but they were vastly inferior to those enjoyed by whites. In the early 1980s, it was estimated that only eight percent of Indian South Africans had completed high school, though the situation is gradually improving. Consequently, there is a considerable gap between

**Sikh soldier**
This late nineteenth-century Sikh soldier was a member of the British colonial armies. His uniform of black, yellow, and white was intended to express racial harmony – though by this time racist polices were in effect in many parts of white-ruled Southern Africa.

educated rich and uneducated poor Indian South Africans. Limited educational opportunities under apartheid and the reservation of many middle-class occupations for whites has meant that an Indian middle class has been slow to develop.

## Social structure

Hindu immigrants brought to South Africa the *caste* system: a strict hierarchy into which a person is born at a certain level that governs marriage, employment, and social status. The vast majority of the indentured laborers were of low caste, however, and very quickly the caste system proved unsustainable in South Africa. Traditional Indian South African family life was based on an extended family system similar to that existing in India. Arranged marriages were the norm and, on marriage, the bride would join the family of her husband and she would come under the authority of her mother-in-law, the female head of household. Since the 1950s, traditional Indian family life has gradually been eroded, social separation of the sexes has largely ceased, and arranged marriages are no longer the norm – social and family life now resemble those of other urban South Africans of similar economic backgrounds.

## Culture and religion

**RELIGION** The majority of Indian South Africans are Hindu, while a minority are Muslim or Christian.

**CLOTHING** For men, Western styles of dress have become the norm. Young women rarely wear the *sari* except, perhaps, on formal occasions, though many older women continue to wear them on a day-to-day basis.

**Soofie Mosque**
This beautiful *mosque* (Muslim place of worship) is a fine example of Islamic architecture in Southern Africa.

© DIAGRAM

# Khoisan

T he name "Khoisan" is a linguistic term for the closely-related Khoikhoi and San peoples. The Khoikhoi (now largely a historical grouping) and the San are also known, sometimes disparagingly, as the Hottentots and the Bushmen respectively. In fact, many of the names used to refer to the various Khoisan groups, including "San," are considered insulting by the Khoisan themselves as they are often derogatory labels given them by other peoples. There are less than 100,000 Khoisan: about 50,000 in Botswana (where they are called Basarwa); 33,000 in Namibia; 8,000 in Angola; 4,500 in South Africa; and 2,000 in Zambia and Zimbabwe.

## History

Descendants of the first known inhabitants of Southern Africa, the Khoisan probably originated in what is now western Zimbabwe and northern Botswana, where they lived in widely-scattered bands at least 20,000 years ago. Around 2,300 years ago, some Khoisan *hunter-gatherers* (people who live on food that can be hunted or collected from the wild instead of growing crops or raising livestock) in northern Botswana began to keep livestock. Over the course of generations, these people migrated

### Khoisan timeline

| | |
|---|---|
| **25,000** **BCE** | Oldest examples of Khoisan rock art in Southern Africa |
| **c. 400s** | Some Khoisan begin to keep livestock: Khoikhoi emerge |
| **200s CE** | Displacement of Khoisan by Bantu-speaking peoples begins |
| **1652** | Dutch settlement of the Cape of Good Hope begins |
| **1657– 1677** | Khoikhoi and Dutch farmers (Boers) fight over land; Khoikhoi pushed out of lands |
| **1713** | Foreign epidemic of smallpox devastates Khoikhoi |
| **1774** | Dutch begin systematic slaughter of Khoikhoi |
| **1799** | Last major Khoikhoi revolt |
| **1806** | British take over Cape |
| **1836– 1848** | Boers on Great Trek with Khoikhoi servants |
| **1884** | Germany colonizes Namibia as South West Africa |
| **1884– 1885** | British colonize Botswana as Bechuanaland |
| **1910** | Union of South Africa formed |
| **1963** | Central Kalahari Game Reserve established in Botswana |
| **1966** | Botswana independent |
| **1980s** | *Droughts* throughout Kalahari |
| **1990** | Namibian independence; 4,000 Namibian Khoisan move to South Africa |
| **1992** | "The First People of the Kalahari" (Khwe Khoisan political movement) founded |
| **1996** | Planned eviction of Khwe from Central Kalahari Game Reserve is delayed pending talks with government |

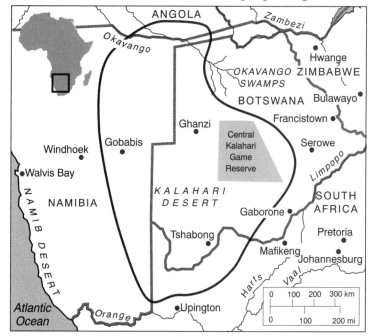

south, reaching the Cape 2,000 years ago and gradually developing into the *pastoralist* (livestock-raising) Khoikhoi people. The Khoikhoi first encountered Europeans in the late fifteenth century, when Portuguese mariners visited the Cape. During the course of the sixteenth century, they regularly traded cattle and sheep for iron goods and beads brought by the sailors. In the seventeenth century, Dutch settlers established farms at the Cape and began expanding onto Khoikhoi grazing lands. Without access to land for their livestock, many Khoikhoi became hunter-gatherers or settled on European-owned farms as laborers. The Dutch farmers (Boers) relied heavily on Khoikhoi labor and bound their workers tightly to them using law, coercion, and force. Although technically free, many Khoikhoi had no choice but to work on Boer farms. Now extinct as a separate ethnic group, descendants of Khoikhoi and Europeans helped form the present-day Cape Colored population.

The San faced similar pressures to those experienced by the Khoikhoi. Throughout Southern Africa they were gradually dispossessed of their hunting grounds – first by migrations of Bantu-speaking peoples into Southern Africa and later by European settlers. Small groups of Bantu-speakers began moving into Southern Africa in the early centuries of the first millennium. The San were either displaced by the more-numerous Bantu peoples and forced to retreat to isolated arid regions or were absorbed into the new societies. The Europeans were harsher and many San were killed on sight by the white settlers. By the nineteenth century, only small bands of San remained in South Africa, living in some of the most arid parts of the northwest Cape. Some San succeeded in fleeing to Botswana and Namibia where they joined long-established San communities, but there, too, they found themselves in competition for land with cattle-raising Tswana, Herero, and other peoples.

**RECENT EVENTS** Many Khoisan were recruited into the Portuguese colonial army in Mozambique and the South African Army in Namibia. After Namibia became independent from South Africa in 1990, however, around 4,000 Khoisan moved to South Africa.

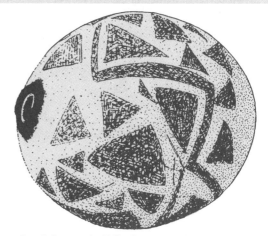

**Ostrich eggshell flask**
For thousands of years, ostrich eggshells have been made into flasks and used by the Khoisan to store water and sometimes food. The eggs can be carried or buried in the ground to provide water in the future. This examples date from the twentieth century and has been elaborately engraved. Today, engraved eggshells are produced for the tourist market throughout Southern Africa.

**Khoisan woman**
The weather-worn face of a Khoisan woman. She is wearing an intricately-beaded headband.

© DIAGRAM

**The Coldstream Stone**
Painted two thousand years ago by a Khoisan artisan, this quartzite stone was excavated from Coldstream Cave on the southern Cape coast. It was found placed on the shoulder of a skeleton and is thought to have played a role in funerary rites.

**Kung healer**
This Khoisan man of the Kung group of northeastern Namibia is healing a pregnant Herero woman. Kung healing involves going into a trancelike state called *kia,* usually reached by performing a particular dance. This activates *num* (an energy originally from the gods), which is then used as a healing force. The Kung's reputation for healing is considerable and attracts many clients who nowadays have to pay for the service.

In recent decades, the Botswana government and cattle herders have systematically driven the Khoisan from most of their territories in the Kalahari Desert. The establishment of the Central Kalahari Game Reserve in 1961 helped safeguard the land rights of some of the local Khoisan – the Khwe. Limited provision of facilities in the area, however, has offset the advantages. After surviving *drought* (inadequate rainfall) in the 1980s, the Khwe now face the threat of relocation. As part of plans to encourage tourism and conserve the environment, the Botswana government announced plans to induce the Khwe to leave the reserve in 1996. Although many are willing to relocate, others are not and they have formed various political groups to put pressure on the government to recognize their rights. The mass relocation has been averted while the government consults with the Khwe.

## Language
Khoisan languages are distinguished by their use of various unique "click" or popping sounds made with the tongue on different parts of the mouth – many of which have been incorporated into other African languages.

## Ways of life
Historically, the main difference between the Khoikhoi and the San was in their lifestyles – the Khoikhoi were chiefly pastoralists and the San purely hunter-gatherers. Both the Khoikhoi and the San lived a largely *nomadic* or *seminomadic* existence, the Khoikhoi herding fat-tailed sheep and long-horned cattle. Those who lived by the coast also gathered shellfish. The Khoisan were noted for their hunting skills and their tracking ability, a skill that was vital both for locating wildlife and for following animals wounded by poisoned arrows.

Today, dispossessed of their land, few Khoisan are solely hunter-gatherers. Many keep livestock (mostly goats and occasionally cattle) and grow crops such as sorghum, corn, sugar cane, melons, and cowpeas. Many Khoisan still forage for wild nuts and plants – as do poor non-Khoisan people – and hunt for meat, particularly during the dry season, to supplement their diet. Giraffes, antelopes, reptiles, and birds provide most of the meat in the Khoisan diet. Although laws in Botswana have greatly restricted their right to hunt game, many take the risk rather than face hunger. Men are usually responsible for hunting the larger animals and women often do most of the foraging. Division of labor by gender varies from group to group though. In Namibia and Botswana, the Khoisan mainly work as farm laborers or domestic servants and live on the fringes of towns.

## Social structure

Historically, the Khoisan lived in bands generally made up of between twenty-five and fifty people related to each other through blood or marriage. Bands had leaders rather than rulers and there was no overall system of government. Discussion and consensus were often the pattern of rule. Food and water were divided according to seniority and property was shared to avoid jealousy.

Most Khoisan now live in mixed settlements that many different ethnic groups call their home. In Botswana, many were forcibly relocated to state-created settlements to make way for cattle herding. Most Khoisan groups have hereditary leadership positions that can be held by a man or a woman. These leaders now have limited official authority but still have some social standing. Hereditary leaders are, however, often elected to state posts such as chairperson of the village development committee or are appointed by local councils to hear minor civil cases.

## Culture and religion

**RELIGION** Khoisan religious beliefs and practices have many features in common between groups but variations exist. The worship of a great and good god (called *Nadi* in the central Kalahari) is common to many groups. Also, there is sometimes an evil being called *Gaua* or *Gawama*, whose mission is to disrupt the good god's work.

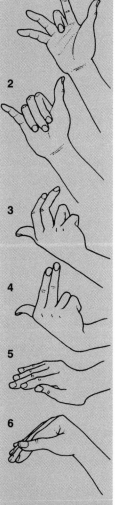

**Khoisan rock art** *(above)*
The Khoisan are famous for their ancient rock paintings, found in caves and on exposed rock surfaces. Many date from thousands of years ago. This painting is relatively recent (probably from within the last 1,500 years) as the larger people on the right are most likely Bantu-speakers, who did not appear in Southern Africa until the first millennium. It seems the Khoisan *(center)* have stolen cattle from the herders.

**Sign language** *(left)*
Hand signals enabled Khoisan hunters to communicate with one another silently while tracking animals.
**Key**
1 Giraffe
2 Bat-eared fox
3 Sable antelope
4 Eland
5 Tortoise
6 Ostrich

© DIAGRAM

# Madagascan peoples

madagascar is a large island – the fourth largest in the world – in the Indian Ocean off the southeast coast of Africa. It has a population of over thirteen million, made up of eighteen principal ethnic groups plus minority groups of Europeans (mainly French nationals), Comorans (from the nearby Comoros Islands), Indians, Pakistanis, and Chinese.

The Madagascan peoples can be divided into two main groups: those of Indonesian descent, who live mainly in the central and south-central highlands of the interior, and those of Black African descent, who inhabit the coastal regions and are sometimes known collectively as the Côtiers (the coastal people).

The most important of the highland peoples are the Merina, who make up about twenty-seven percent of the island's thirteen million population, and the Betsileo (thirteen percent of the population). The major coastal

## Madagascan peoples timeline

| | |
|---|---|
| upto 1000 | Indonesians arrive on island of Madagascar |
| 1400 | Muslim trading colonies and kingdoms established |
| 1500s | Sakalava kingdom established |
| 1600s | Tsitambala confederation |
| 1700s | Betsimisaraka kingdom emerges from Tsitambala confederation |
| 1791 | Fall of Betsimisaraka kingdom |
| 1797 | Unified Merina kingdom in existence |
| 1810– 1828 | Reign of Merina king Radama I, island unification and opening up to foreign influences begins |
| 1822 | Sakalava kingdom collapses |
| 1883– 1885 | Franco-Merina War over control of island |
| 1895 | French rule begins |
| 1958 | Semiautonomous Malagasy Republic established |
| 1960 | Malagasy Republic independent |
| 1975 | Malagasy renamed Madagascar |
| 1993 | Free elections end eighteen years of dictatorship |

## The peoples of Madagascar

The map on the right shows the locations of the eighteen principal ethnic groups of Madagascar, who are listed below in order of decreasing size.

| | |
|---|---|
| 1 Merina | 10 Bara |
| 2 Betsimisaraka | 11 Sihanaka |
| 3 Betsileo | 12 Antanosy |
| 4 Tsimihety | 13 Mahafaly |
| 5 Sakalava | 14 Antaifasy |
| 6 Antandroy | 15 Makoa |
| 7 Antaisaka | 16 Bezanozano |
| 8 Tanala | 17 Antankarana |
| 9 Antaimoro | 18 Antambahoaka |

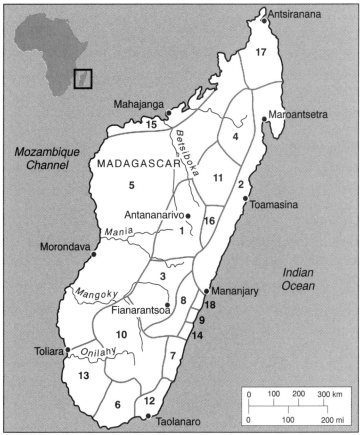

peoples include the Betsimisaraka, the Antandroy, and the Sakalava. These peoples represent about fifteen, eight, and six percent of the total population respectively. The Merina, Betsimisaraka, and Betsileo each number over one million people.

## History

The first people to settle in Madagascar were of Malayo-Polynesian origin. They arrived on the island from Indonesia between 2,000 and 1,500 years ago, and over the following centuries they were joined by waves of immigrants from Africa, Asia, Arabia, and Europe.

**THREE GREAT KINGDOMS** Madagascar's history is dominated by three large, powerful kingdoms, formed by the unification of smaller states. The first of these was the Sakalava kingdom – established along the west coast in the late sixteenth century. By the middle of the eighteenth century it controlled nearly half the island, but began to fragment after the death of its last ruler, Queen Ravahiny, in 1808. The second had its origins in the Tsitambala confederation, a seventeenth-century alliance of chiefdoms along the east coast. This confederation was taken over and expanded in the early eighteenth century by Ratsimilaho, an English-educated son of an English pirate, who created from it the Betsimisaraka kingdom. The third great kingdom emerged in the central highlands during the fifteenth century, when the Merina settled there and subjugated the original inhabitants, the Vazimba. The Merina kingdom grew and prospered and, after the fall of the Betsimisaraka kingdom in 1791 and the Sakalava kingdom in 1822, it controlled most of the island.

**COLONIALISM** European contact with the island began with the arrival of a Portuguese fleet in 1500. For the next three hundred years, the Portuguese, British, Dutch, and French tried to set up colonies on the island. These early colonies were repeatedly destroyed by the islanders, but they tolerated small bases that were set up in the late seventeenth century by pirates from Europe and the American colonies, who preyed on shipping in the Indian Ocean.

**Mother and child**
This Malagasy woman is carrying her baby in a makeshift pocket of her *lamba* – a wraparound dress. The lamba is a very traditional style of clothing and was once worn by people of all the principal ethnic groups of Madagascar. Today, the lamba is rarely worn.

**King Radama I** *(below)*
Son and successor of Andrianampoinimerina, Radama I ruled over the Merina kingdom from 1810 until his death in 1828. He extended Merina control over most of the island. Radama was succeeded by his wife, Queen Ranavalona, who continued the subjugation of the island.

© DIAGRAM

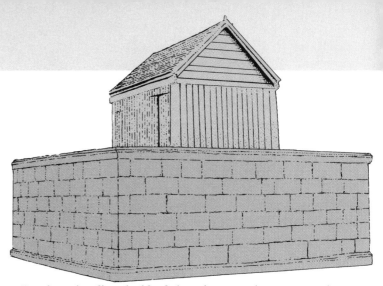

## Tomb

This tomb of a noble family consists of a burial vault with a prayer house on top. Tombs can be seen dotted all over Madagascar's countryside. Originally a Merina custom, many peoples now build tombs for their dead. Often the focus of ceremonies and festivals, ancestral tombs signify a person's place in society and their rights to land – without a tomb a person is a nobody. Since World War II, tombs have been built with cement-finished sides and painted designs. The cost of this, however, has lead to a revival of more-traditional, affordable forms.

## Wooden figure

Mystery surrounds this nineteenth-century wooden sculpture. The top half of a post, it may have been used as a tomb sculpture (by the Mahafaly) or as a *hazomanga* (a village ritual post) by the Sakalava. It has been attributed to many different Malagasy peoples at one time or another. This sculpture was a source of inspiration for the American sculptor Sir Jacob Epstein.

During the first half of the nineteenth century, the Merina ruler King Radama I opened up Madagascar to outside influences, particularly French and British. In 1817, the British acknowledged him as king of all Madagascar, and British and other European advisors began helping him establish schools, industries, and a professional army and set up Christian churches. These policies were reversed when Radama died, in 1828, and was succeeded by his wife, Queen Ranavalona I. She forced most of the Europeans from the country and closed the schools and churches, but the French and British began to return after her death in 1861.

Over the next thirty years, France, Britain, and the Merina argued over which of them should control the island, and there was war between the Merina and the French from 1883 to 1885. In 1890, Britain agreed to let France have Madagascar in return for control of Egypt and Zanzibar, and the country was declared a French *protectorate* (colony) in 1895. This was opposed by the queen, Ranavalona II, and by the people, so the French imposed their rule by force.

**INDEPENDENCE** Madagascar remained a French colony until 1960, when it regained its independence under its first president, Philibert Tsiranana. French influence remained strong under Tsiranana's right-wing rule, but ended when he was forced to resign after an anti-government uprising in 1972. The army commander, General Gabriel Ramanantsoa, then took control of the government and closed the French military bases on the island. Ramanantsoa was forced out in 1975, but his successor, Colonel Richard Ratsimandrava, was shot dead within a week of seizing power by an army group who staged a military takeover. In turn, this group was defeated by another military faction and Didier Ratsiraka, formerly the country's foreign minister, became president and set the country on a socialist path. The country, which since 1958 had been known as the Malagasy Republic, was renamed the Democratic Republic of Madagascar.

**RECENT EVENTS** Demonstrations, a general strike, and pressure from France in 1991 and 1992 forced presidential elections in which Ratsiraka was defeated by Professor Albert Zafy, leader of the opposition alliance Forces Vives. A general election in 1993 was won by Forces Vives and, two months later, the Madagascan parliament elected Francisque Ravony as prime minister of the country.

## Languages

The official languages of Madagascar are Malagasy and French, but less than thirty percent of the population can speak French – outside of the cities, most people speak only Malagasy. The different ethnic groups speak various dialects of the Malagasy language, which is a member of the Western Austronesian language family. Standard Malagasy (the "official" form) is used to bridge the gap between dialects; it is based on the Merina dialect and written in the Roman alphabet.

   The minority populations such as the Indians, Europeans, Chinese, and Arabs speak either an Indian or European language, Chinese, or Arabic respectively – usually in addition to Malagasy.

## Ways of life

**AGRICULTURE** Outside of the main towns and cities, the way of life is mostly agricultural and so is heavily influenced by climate and geography. In the hot and humid tropical climate of

**Antanosy granary** (above)
This raised wooden structure would have been used by the Antanosy as a *granary* (a place to store grain). Wooden disks on the supporting pillars stop rats destroying the stores.

**Wooden spoon** (right)
Throughout Madagascar, sculpted wooden spoons are used for serving rice on special occasions. This spoon has been attributed to the Sakalava people.

**Betsileo hairstyle** (left)
This Betsileo woman has her hair braided and looped into an attractive arrangement. Hairstyles vary according to the current fashions.

© DIAGRAM

## Bamboo

This woman is carrying two large bamboo poles. On the east coast of Madagascar the climate is very hot and damp. These are ideal conditions for growing bamboo, which has a great variety of uses.

## Betsimisaraka house (below)

This Betsimisaraka house has been built with bamboo and has a thatched roof.

the north and east, important crops include coffee, vanilla, cloves, fruit, and sugar cane. The hot coastal plains of the west and southwest are drier than the north and east, and their main products are rice, cotton, tobacco, and cassava. Livestock is raised in the arid south of the country, the temperate highland regions of the interior, and on the coastal plains. Cattle are often regarded as indicators of wealth and not as sources of income. The highlands are important rice-growing areas but have been badly affected by soil erosion and *deforestation*. Fishing is important in many areas, both along the coast and in the numerous rivers and lakes.

Most farmers practice *subsistence agriculture*, in which people grow food for their own consumption, but some crops, such as tobacco, coffee, and vanilla, are grown to be sold for cash. The work involved is usually divided between men and women. For example, men typically prepare the ground for planting, build the houses and cattle pens, hunt, and fish. Women usually tend the crops, grow herbs and vegetables, and do domestic tasks such as cooking and laundry.

**TRADE AND INDUSTRY** Only a relatively small proportion of people are involved in industry, and the majority of these work in food processing plants. Textiles, brewing, and paper and soap production are other important sectors. Sea fishing, by coastal fisherman, is in the process of being industrialized. The Indian population largely dominates the jewelry and textile trades. On the east coast, the Chinese community is largely engaged in small-scale banking and the trading of agricultural products. Others work in tourism – Madagascar's many unique plants and animals and diversity of environments attract a considerable number of tourists to the island.

## Social structure

**SOCIAL STRUCTURE** Family and *clan* relationships are very important in Madagascan society. The members of a clan trace their origins back to a common and revered ancestor. Marriage customs vary from one ethnic group to another. Although most marriages are between one man and one woman, the customs of some people allow a man to have more than one wife, while others allow a woman to have more than one husband.

**POLITICAL STRUCTURE** Politically, Madagascar is divided into six provinces and each of these is further divided into administrative districts down to village level. A typical village is governed by its male and female elders led by the senior male.

## Culture and religion

**RELIGION** About fifty percent of the population of Madagascar follow the Malagasy religion, which is based on reverence for spirits and ancestors. This is expressed in regular ceremonies centered on the ancestral tombs, which are built and maintained with great care. These ceremonies help people to maintain a feeling of identity with each other and with their past, and, whenever possible, the dead are always buried in their ancestral tombs. Often, aspects of the Malagasy religion (such as ancestor reverence) are practiced in conjunction with Christianity or Islam.

Christianity was brought to Madagascar by European missionaries during the nineteenth century and today about forty percent of the population are Christian. The Christians in the interior of the country, where the British had most influence, are mainly Protestant. Those in the coastal regions, where French influence was stronger, are mostly Catholic.

The third major religion of Madagascar is Islam. This is followed by around ten percent of the population, and was brought to the island by Arab, East African, and Comoran traders who began to trade there in the ninth century. These traders, who were mostly *Sunni* Muslims, also brought with them a tradition of *divination*, or prophecy, called *sikidy*. Although the majority of Madagascar's Muslims belong to the *Sunni* branch of Islam, there are also a number of *Shiite* and *Ismaili* Muslims on the island, most of whom are of Indian or Pakistani origin.

**Mpsikidy** (above)
Among the Sakalava, there are religious practitioners called *mpsikidy*. These are basically *diviners* who diagnose and attempt to heal particular ills or foretell the future. In this example, a mpisikidy is using seeds to tell his client's future. The seeds are shuffled into sixteen small piles and the arrangements of shapes formed are then interpreted by the diviner.

**Mahafaly tomb sculpture**
This wooden sculpted pole was produced for the tomb of a Mahafaly of some standing. Known as *aloalo,* up to thirty of such poles can appear on on the top of one tomb. More recent aloalo often incorporate figures such as airplanes and buses above the semicircular and circular shapes, which are thought to represent the Moon and half-Moon. The sculptures are both commemorative of the deceased and symbolic of the link that ancestors provide between the dead and the living.

© DIAGRAM

# Music: jazz, roots, and mbira

**Ladysmith Black Mambazo**

The South African group Ladysmith Black Mambazo, led by Joseph Shabalala, released their first album in 1973 and it became the first African LP to sell over 25,000 copies. It was their work with Paul Simon in the mid-1980s, however, that helped to make *iscathamiya* the most widely-recognized South African music style.

**Mbira**

In Zimbabwe, the *mbira* (or thumb piano) is an instrument that forms the basis of the music, chanting, and dancing of the ceremonies at which the Shona make contact with the spirit world.

**Thomas Mapfumo**

Mapfumo is well known for his *electric mbira* style, which translates the sounds of the *mbira* into guitar riffs. He is outspoken about political matters and his 1990s single *Corruption* sparked controversy in Zimbabwe.

*The music of Southern Africa is vibrant and varied, blending traditional harmonies, rhythms, and instruments with modern music styles, such as blues and jazz, to create new and exciting musical forms.*

## Mbaqanga and iscathamiya

*As might be expected given its size and dominance, South Africa is the leading musical influence in the region and has produced many unique forms such as the* mbaqanga *songs of the* townships, *and the powerful Zulu a capella (unaccompanied) singing style,* iscathamiya. *The ancestry of the mbaqanga vocal style can be traced back to the four-part harmonies of 1950s African-American bands. South African musicians at first copied these harmonies, but then Africanized them by adding an extra voice, creating a five-part-harmony style that echoed traditional African singing. The Zulu iscathamiya style originated in the all-male workers' hostels of the industrial areas of 1920s Natal. Typified these days by bands such as Ladysmith Black Mambazo, it features unaccompanied close-harmony vocals and sophisticated dance routines.*

## South African jazz

*The post-World War II era saw the growing popularity of jazz music in South African urban areas – Johannesburg in particular boasted many bands with large followings. Township jazz bands combined American swing with* marabi *(or jive music – an early form of township jazz based around three chords) to create the dynamic African jazz style. In the 1960s, a more self-consciously-artistic style called progressive jazz emerged, often with an overtly antiapartheid stance. Musicians such as trumpeter Hugh Masekela and pianist Dollar Brand (who became Abdullah Ibrahim) were at the forefront of this movement. Oppressive government policies sadly forced many of this era's best musicians into exile, ending the golden age of*

*South African jazz. In the last few years, however, the end of apartheid and the return of many exiled musicians has revitalized the jazz scene and new styles and faces are emerging.*

## Mbira, chimurenga, and rumbira

*Zimbabwe has also made important contributions to Southern African music, often with styles influenced by the* mbira *(thumb piano). Although the mbira is traditionally played by men, some of its most prominent players today are women, such as Beulah Diago and Stella Chiweshe. In 1970s, the powerful, hypnotic style of the mbira inspired a unique contemporary music style called* chimurenga. *Created by Thomas Mapfumo,* chimurenga — *which means "liberation war" — played an important role in the struggle for majority rule in Zimbabwe. During that time, its Shona and Ndebele lyrics contained messages of resistance that few whites could understand but which helped to raise the morale of the liberation movement.*

*Other distinctive mbira-influenced Zimbabwean music forms are* Jit Jive *(a term coined by the internationally successful Bhundu Boys), an energetic dance music featuring mbira-style guitars, and* rumbira, *an exciting blend of electric mbira and Zairean rumba rhythms.*

## Roots revival

*Electric-roots music — combining modern instruments such as electric guitars and synthesizers with traditional instruments and vocals — is a popular modern genre in Southern Africa. Previously marginalized by Western-style pop, Madagascar's music has been undergoing a roots revival in the last few years. Jean Emilien, for example, blends traditional* vako-drazana *songs with dance music and plays an amplified version of the guitarlike* kabosy, *while Ricky Randimbiarison plays* vakojazzana, *combining vako-drazana and jazz.*

**Hugh Masekela** *(above)*
After spending over three decades in exile in the US and elsewhere, Masekela's music has expanded to include influences from African-American funk and soul as well as from *marabi* and *mbaqanga* music.

**Miriam Makeba** *(above left)*
Miriam Makeba is probably the best-known singer to emerge from the golden age of South African jazz. Exiled in 1963 for her antiapartheid views, she has now returned to South Africa. Her singing style incorporates the "click" sounds used in many Southern African languages.

**Valiha horn** *(left)*
Consisting of a long bamboo tube with twenty strings stretched lengthwise around its circumference, the *valiha* is considered the national instrument of Madagascar. Still popular with modern musicians, valihas are now being made in different materials, metal strings are used, and a thirty-eight-stringed chromatic model has even been designed.

**Tarika** *(below)*
Tarika are one of the bands at the forefront of the roots-revival movement in Madagascar.

# Ndebele and Matabele

The Ndebele live in the Transvaal province of South Africa. They are commonly divided into two separate groups: the Northern Ndebele and the Southern Ndebele. The Southern Ndebele are subdivided into two main branches: the Ndzundza and the Manala, which take their names from early leaders. The Northern Ndebele have been absorbed into the Sotho population and are no longer considered a distinct ethnic group.

The Matabele live in a region of southern Zimbabwe called Matabeleland. They are sometimes, confusingly, called Ndebele as well – the Ndebele and Matabele both refer to themselves as amaNdebele. The histories and cultures of the Ndebele and the Matabele are closely connected and the two groups are often treated as branches of the same, Ndebele, people. The Ndebele number about 500,000 and the Matabele about 4,000,000.

## History

**NDEBELE** The Ndebele story begins with the Nguni, a Bantu-speaking people who arrived in Southern Africa around the 200s. The Ndebele of today are one of many ethnic groups descended from the original Nguni settlers.

### Ndebele and Matabele timeline

| | |
|---|---|
| **200s** | Bantu-speaking peoples begin to arrive in Southern Africa |
| **1500s** | Ndebele groups emerge |
| **1700s** | Southern Ndebele fragment |
| **1819– 1839** | *Mfecane/Difaqane*: period of mass migrations and wars |
| **1820s** | Mizilikazi founds Ndebele state |
| **1836– 1848** | Great Trek brings Boers into conflict with people inland |
| **1837** | Mizilikazi and followers move north |
| **c. 1840** | Mabhogo's reign over Ndzundza Ndebele begins |
| **1883** | Ndebele conquered by Boers |
| **1890** | British South Africa Company colonizes Southern Rhodesia |
| **1896** | Shona and Matabele at war with British colonizers |
| **1910** | White-minority ruled Union of South Africa created |
| **1923** | British government takes control of Southern Rhodesia; white immigration encouraged |
| **1948** | *Apartheid* begins in South Africa |
| **1965** | Illegal white-minority rule established in Southern Rhodesia as Rhodesia |
| **1967– 1975** | Period of guerrilla warfare against white Rhodesians |
| **1980** | Rhodesia independent as Zimbabwe; one-party state emerges |
| **1982** | Antigovernment terrorism and violence in Matabeleland |
| **1991** | Zimbabwean single–party system abandoned. Apartheid officially ends in South Africa |
| **1994** | First nonracial elections are held in South Africa |

("Ndebele" is the Sotho name for "Nguni.") History suggests that they probably split off some time in the late 1500s under a chief named Musi. Early on, the Ndebele split into two groups – Northern and Southern – most of whom migrated from present-day KwaZulu/Natal northward to modern Transvaal, where the Northern Ndebele gradually became absorbed by their Sotho neighbors. In the 1700s, the Southern Ndebele fragmented into different groups. Two branches survived this fragmentation into the present day: a smaller group, led by Manala, and a larger group, led by Ndzundza.

The Ndzundza Ndebele reached a height of prosperity in the mid-nineteenth century under the rule of King Mabhogo, but they were finally conquered by the Boers' South African Republic (Transvaal) in 1883. All the Ndzundza lands were confiscated and the people forced to work for the Boers (Afrikaner farmers) virtually as slaves. After the Union of South Africa was created in 1910, the Ndebele came under white-minority rule.

**MATABELE** The Matabele are also descended from early Nguni settlers, but did not emerge as an independent people until the nineteenth century. In the early 1800s, South Africa was dominated by the Zulu led by Shaka. His lieutenant was Mzilikazi, one of the Khumalo, an Ndebele group who had not migrated to the Transvaal but remained in present-day KwaZulu/Natal. In 1823, Mzilikazi rebelled against Shaka during the violent *Mfecane/Difaqane* era and led the Khumalo northward to safety. Mzilikazi settled north of the Vaal River and established a powerful (Ndebele) kingdom near present-day Pretoria. This kingdom was attacked repeatedly by Zulu, Griqua, and Kora people and finally by Boers on the Great Trek. In 1837, Mzilikazi led his people to a new settlement that he called Bulawayo ("Great Place"), which is where they came to be known as the Matabele.

The Matabele came into conflict with the British in the late 1800s when the British South Africa Company, headed by the imperialist Cecil Rhodes, occupied most of the region. In 1890, the Matabele found themselves the second-largest ethnic group in a British-dominated territory called Southern Rhodesia, for Rhodes.

**Beadwork doll**
Ndebele women produce a great variety of beaded items, including bottles, gourds, dolls – such as the one below – and clothing.

**Ndebele woman**
This Ndebele woman is wearing a beaded apron and a blanket. Many women wear copper, brass, or beaded necklaces, rings, and leg rings. Ndebele women are more likely to be seen wearing traditional-style clothes than Ndebele men.

© DIAGRAM

**Mapoto** *(opposite above)*
This beaded apron is called a *mapoto* and would have been worn by a married woman. It dates from the mid-1900s and would be considered old-fashioned by the Ndebele today. Modern beadwork clothes use a variety of colors, often on a white background. The designs reflect current fashions and incorporate modern motifs. Originally, the beads used were glass and were sewn onto leather; today, canvas bases, plastic beads, and fabric braids are also used.

**Beaded hoops**
Beaded hoops are often worn by married women on their legs, necks, and arms. They are made from bundles of dried grass shaped into circles, bound tightly, and then encrusted with beads and other decorative items such as the brass buttons this woman has used. Since the 1920s, neck hoops have grown in size and can now be up to 8 in. (20 cm) wide.

**RECENT EVENTS** In 1973, under *apartheid* (the racist doctrine of "separate development") the Ndebele were given a *homeland* called KwaNdebele, which was in lands completely strange to them. Great conflict arose in the 1980s between the government-appointed regime of the homeland and the supporters of the Ndebele monarch: 160 died; 300 were detained; and hundreds simply disappeared. The homelands were abolished, in 1994, following the ending of apartheid legislation in 1991.

Meanwhile, the Matabele experienced years of oppression at the hands of the white-minority governments of Southern Rhodesia and Rhodesia. After a prolonged guerrilla war, majority rule was introduced with the birth of the independent state of Zimbabwe in 1980. Even after independence, the Matabele suffered the effects of a power struggle between the leaders of two former rebel groups: Robert Mugabe – the new prime minister – and Joshua Nkomo, whose opposition party drew most of its support from Matabeleland. Government reprisals against dissidents in Matabeleland were harsh and culminated in a very brutal massacre in 1987. An amnesty declared in 1988 has eased the situation.

## Language
The language of both the Ndebele and the Matabele is called Ndebele (or isiNdebele).

## Ways of Life
The ways of life of both the Ndebele and the Matabele people are still greatly affected by the legacy of white-minority rule. In South Africa and Rhodesia, the best farming land was allocated to whites and, despite land redistribution plans in independent Zimbabwe and the end of apartheid in South Africa, the situation has not improved greatly. Most Matabele households rely on food-crop farming augmented by the sale of cash crops and surplus produce; on casual employment; money sent by family members working as migrant laborers; and wages from working as farm laborers. Today, the majority of Ndebele work for wages in a variety of jobs including farm labor, but some with

access to land still farm. Even today, some Ndebele farm laborers work under the same conditions as they did in the 1880s for the Boers and still do not receive any wages. The main food crops grown are corn, wheat, millet, and sorghum as well as, in South Africa, pumpkins, beans, and potatoes. In Zimbabwe, the main cash crops are cotton, tobacco, and sugar. Matabele farmers in Zimbabwe are still recovering from the effects of the 1991–2 *drought*.

## Social structure

**SOCIAL STRUCTURE** Families are based on men as heads of households and in the country three generations often share the same home or live close together. Because so many Ndebele women, as well as men, go to distant parts to work, grandparents frequently bring up the children. Inheritance of property generally passes to the youngest son. A man may still have more than one wife, though having only one wife is the general rule in South Africa. A woman, however, can have only one husband.

**POLITICAL STRUCTURE** Historically, the Ndebele and Matabele were ruled by kings and paramount chiefs, and vestiges of this system remain today. Chiefs retain some authority, but they have to work within the modern systems of government in both countries. Justice was administered by a group's local court, and some disputes are still settled in this way.

## Culture and religion

**RELIGION** The majority of Ndebele are Christians, most have converted since the emergence of the many independent African-run Christian churches. Certain features of the Ndebele religion are still widely followed. The most important of these, is belief in *amaNdlozi,* the revered ancestors of the family who are also believed to be spirit guardians. The Ndebele also maintain their beliefs in healing through spiritual forces. This is carried out by *sangomas* (*diviners*), who may be men or women, and *nyangas* (essentially herbalists), who are always men.

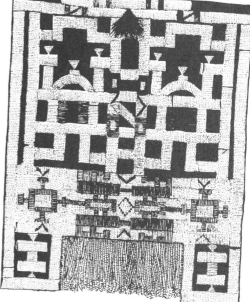

**Mural art** *(below)*
The walls of this house have been decorated with murals. Ndebele women have become famous for the geometric designs with which they paint their houses. The custom probably originated in the eighteenth century but has undergone an explosion in popularity since the 1940s. Initially, paints were made from clay, ash, and dung and natural pigments were used to create earthy colors – still seen in some rural areas. Today, brightly-colored, commercially-produced paints are used. Earlier designs incorporated mainly chevron and triangular shapes. More recent designs also incorporate shapes of airplanes, lightbulbs, and other modern influences on Ndebele life. Some women are privately commissioned to paint on canvas or to decorate shopping centers and even cars.

© DIAGRAM

# Ovambo

The Ovambo are concentrated on the high, flat, stoneless plains between the Kunene (Cunene) and Okavango (Cubango) Rivers in the far north of Namibia and the far south of Angola. The 150,000 Angolan Ovambo are one of that country's smaller ethnic groups, but the half million Namibian Ovambo constitute almost half of Namibia's population. Many Ovambo have migrated to live elsewhere in Namibia where they work, either on a permanent or temporary basis, on farms, in mines, and as civil servants. Due to the policy of *apartheid* ("separate development") and South Africa's policy of "divide and rule," many people have come to reject being labeled "Ovambo," instead preferring to be identified simply as "Namibian."

## History

It is believed that the Ovambo migrated to their present homeland from the northeast – in the area of present-day Zambia – sometime around the fifteenth or sixteenth centuries. The Ovambo have a close cultural and historical relationship with the Herero who live farther south: legend states that the two peoples are descended from brothers who parted when they reached the present home of the Ovambo – Ovamboland.

## Ovambo timeline

| | |
|---|---|
| **c. 1500s** | Ovambo arrive in Namibia |
| **1500s** | Portuguese establish colony in present-day Angola |
| **1884** | Germany colonizes Namibia as South West Africa; Christianity introduced to the region |
| **1915** | German South West Africa occupied by South Africa |
| **1920s–1930s** | Numerous Ovambo rebellions quashed by South Africa |
| **1948** | Form of *apartheid* introduced to South West Africa |
| **1950s–1960s** | Main Angolan independence movements formed |
| **1960** | South West Africa People's Organization (SWAPO) founded |
| **1966** | Conflict between SWAPO and South African troops begins |
| **1969** | South Africa's occupation of South West Africa declared illegal by United Nations |
| **1973** | "Independent" Ovamboland *homeland* created in South West Africa |
| **1974** | Portuguese revolution; Angola promised independence |
| **1975** | Civil war breaks out in Angola. Autocratic Ovamboland ruler Filemon Elifas assassinated |
| **1989** | Apartheid legislation repealed in South West Africa |
| **1990** | Namibia independent. Peace accord in Angola |
| **1992** | Civil war in Angola resumes |
| **1994** | Stretch of Namibian-Angolan border closed |
| **1995** | Fragile peace in Angola |

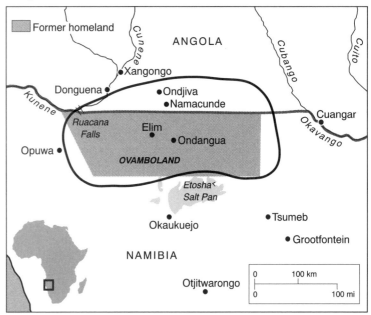

© DIAGRAM

**COLONIALISM** In 1884, Namibia became a colony of Germany, but because of difficulties in controlling the smaller Herero and Nama population to the south, the Germans never took much interest in the areas of Ovambo territory under their jurisdiction. In 1915, Namibia (as South West Africa) – and with it much of Ovamboland – came under South African administration. The South Africans took more interest in Ovamboland, and in the 1920s and 1930s they crushed numerous Ovambo rebellions. The Portuguese had occupied the Angolan coast since the late fifteenth century, but until they ruthlessly asserted their claims to part of southern Angola in the early twentieth century they took little interest in the isolated Ovamboland.

**APARTHEID** South Africa's policy of apartheid, introduced in 1948, was also forced on Namibia. In 1973, Ovamboland was declared "independent" by South Africa. This independence was rejected by the overwhelming majority of Ovambo and by the international community. An assembly of mainly South African-appointed chiefs was created. The Chief Minister, Filemon Elifas, was assassinated in 1975 for his brutal reign of fear, which was backed by the South African army and police. Absences from Ovamboland were allowed only with a work permit – and then without any accompanying family members. Frustration with this system and with the lack of opportunities in Ovamboland, resulting from overpopulation and overgrazing, led to the development of an Ovambo workers' movement.

**INDEPENDENCE** In 1960, the South West Africa People's Organization (SWAPO) emerged from the opposition to South African rule. After more than twenty years of armed struggle, SWAPO led Namibia to independence in 1990. Although SWAPO has been accused by its opposition of being dominated by Ovambo, it upholds strong nontribal and nonracial principles. Ovambo, however, do make up almost half Namibia's population and Ovamboland was in the frontline of the guerrilla war, so it is not surprising that many of the organization's members and leaders are Ovambo.

## Ovamboland (previous page)

Visitors to Ovamboland over one hundred years ago remarked on its cultivated fields surrounded by lush forests. Today, most of these trees have been cut down. The creation of a *homeland* for the Ovambo; the loss of the most fertile farming land to white settlers during the German and then South African colonial eras; refugees from the war in Angola; and Namibia's own independence struggle have all served to deplete the natural environment.

## Omakipa (left)

These ivory clasp-buttons date from the 1930s. Perforations at the back allow the buttons to be attached to belts, strands of beads, or straps that are worn loose. It is an Ovambo custom for a bridegroom to give *omakipa* to his bride on their wedding day. After marriage, the husband would add to his wife's collection, which she would wear on special occasions. Today, buttons such as these are more likely to be family heirlooms than wedding gifts. Omakipa like these are no longer made as it is now illegal to hunt elephants for ivory.

## Ovambo village (right)

Stockades of tall poles surround this settlement and create pathways inside that join the *compounds* together. The open central area is used as a gathering place. This small village contains only around twenty homes.

# Language

The Ovambo are a Bantu-speaking people whose main language is Ovambo, also called Ambo. There are linguistic differences between Ovambo subgroups, but their dialects are easily mutually intelligible.

## Ways of life

**AGRICULTURE** The northern part of Ovamboland is open wooded grassland and the south is more arid grassland. It is subject to two to three months a year of heavy rain that causes widespread flooding of the silt-covered plain, followed by nine or ten months of *drought*. To adapt to these harsh conditions, the Ovambo have taken advantage of what resources are available. Cultivation is largely the preserve of women. The staple crop is millet, pounded into flour and eaten in the form of a dry porridge, while corn is produced for making beer. Beans, sweet potatoes, *groundnuts* (peanuts), melons, and pumpkins are also cultivated. Men tend the livestock: cattle and goats are raised, but, due to flooding, local grazing conditions are not as favorable as they are to the south in Herero territory.

**MIGRANT LABOR** Since the late nineteenth century, Ovambo men have traveled south to work in Namibia's mines or on the railroads, while many women have left Ovamboland to work as domestic servants.

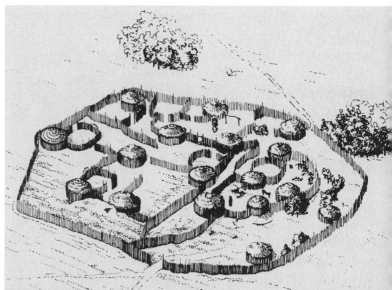

**HOUSING** Most Ovambo live in *compounds* (a linked group of houses) completely encircled by a fence. Husbands, wives, young men and women, and visitors all live in separate buildings. Encircling the compound is a cattle enclosure, which also includes safe storage areas for grain and other goods.

## Social structure

A special feature of Ovambo society is its *matrilineal* succession (descent is traced from mother to daughter). Children are inherited from their mother or their maternal aunts and uncles. Only mothers are considered to be the immediate relations of their children as suggested by the Ovambo proverb "The family does not come from the penis"; the closest relative a father had was his own sister. A husband, wife, their children, and any elders, make up the basic family unit, but the maternal uncle is regarded as the family leader and so he is accorded great respect.

Despite this matrilineal inheritance, official positions are the preserve of men. Social status depends on a man's ancestry, age, and number of cattle. Historically, the ruling elite had the means to survive extended periods of drought and build up grain stocks as well as distribute aid to the poor, thereby earning prestige.

## Culture and religion

**RELIGION** The Finnish Missionary Society has had a continuous presence in Ovamboland since 1870 and its missionaries have established schools, clinics, and churches. The first baptisms took place in 1883. Most Ovambo are now members of the Lutheran Ovambokavango Church; a minority in Namibia are Anglicans and, in Angola, a minority are Catholics.

**ARTS AND CRAFTS** The western Ovambo groups have developed a reputation for their skills in copper and ironworking, making practical implements such as knives and hoes. As there are no iron or copper deposits in Ovamboland, it is assumed that the Ovambo knew the art of smelting iron before they settled in their present lands. Apart from metalworking, other major handicrafts include pottery and basketry.

**Fishing**
Fish are an important part of the Ovambo diet – often eaten dried, powdered, and mixed with *durra* (sorghum) as flavoring. These women are catching fish trapped in the shallows with *shikuki* – reed baskets that have an opening in the top so that when a fish is trapped inside, the fisherwoman can put her hand in to remove the fish.

**Subterranean potter**
Working underground to ensure that the pots dry evenly, this woman is preparing her pots to be fired.

© DIAGRAM

# Shona

The lands of the Shona people cover most of Zimbabwe and extend into Mozambique; there are also Shona populations in South Africa, Botswana, and Zambia. They are the dominant ethnic group in Zimbabwe, where the Shona population of over eight million makes up about seventy percent of the total. Around 500,000 Shona people live outside Zimbabwe, mainly in neighboring countries.

## History

The Shona are descended from Iron-Age, Bantu-speaking farmers who settled on the Zimbabwe plateau in around 200. Little is known of these early settlers except that they worked with iron. From about the tenth century, however, the Shona civilization that had developed in the area became adept at working with gold and copper, both of which were found on the plateau, and traded those metals with coastal cities. The people who ruled this trade became the wealthy elite, the graves of whom were found to contain gold ornaments and imported beads and cloth.

**ZIMBABWES** From around the late 1100s, the Shona began to construct impressive dry-wall enclosures (built without mortar) serving as palaces and called *zimbabwes* (literally, "stone houses"). This building system was perfected at

| Shona timeline | |
|---|---|
| **200s** | Bantu-speaking peoples begin to arrive in Southern Africa |
| **900s** | Bambandyanalo/Mapungubwe trading center on Limpopo River |
| **1000s** | Major Iron-Age settlement, Leopard Kopje, built |
| **1100– 1300** | Bambandyanalo/ Mapungubwe at height |
| **1100s** | Great Zimbabwe building begins |
| **1300s– 1400s** | Great Zimbabwe reaches height; wealth boosted by gold trade |
| **1480** | Mutapa Empire breaks up; Rozvi dynasty emerges |
| **by 1500** | Great Zimbabwe abandoned; Shona civilization moves north to create Mutapa Empire |
| **1700s** | Rozvi Empire fragments |
| **1890** | Cecil Rhodes' British South Africa Company establishes colony of Southern Rhodesia |
| **1896** | Shona and Matabele at war with British colonizers |
| **1923** | British government takes control of Southern Rhodesia; white immigration encouraged |
| **1965** | Illegal white-minority rule established in Southern Rhodesia as Rhodesia |
| **1967– 1975** | Guerrilla war fought against white Rhodesians |
| **1980** | End of white-minority rule in Rhodesia, which is renamed Zimbabwe. One-party state emerges |
| **1991** | Zimbabwean single-party system abandoned |
| **1990s** | *Drought* hits Zimbabwe |
| **1994** | Government corruption scandal |

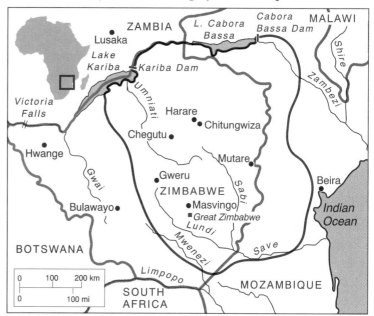

the site of Great Zimbabwe (south of modern Masvingo) from the 1300s onward. Great Zimbabwe had been abandoned as a palace by the Shona kings by the end of the fifteenth century, but it continued as a religious and ceremonial site. The capital was moved north to the area around the Zambezi River. This marked the beginning of a new Shona dynasty, the Mwene Mutapas. The first Mwene Mutapa was Nyatsimba Mutota, who conquered territory from the Kalahari Desert to the Indian Ocean. After the death in 1480 of his successor, Matope, the kingdom split, the southern part being dominated by the Rozvi peoples, a Shona subgroup.

When the Rozvi Empire finally collapsed in the early nineteenth century, over a hundred small Shona states took its place. Many of these were disrupted after 1820 as a result of the wave of emigration emanating from Shaka's Zulu *Mfecane* expansion. This brought the Matabele people into southern Zimbabwe. It was the Matabele who gave these many groups the name "Shona." Previously, each group was known by its own name, even though they were all Shona-speaking peoples.

**COLONIALISM** After 1850, most of the area was colonized by the British and renamed Southern Rhodesia, for the British imperialist and colonial administrator Cecil Rhodes. In 1965, the white population declared independence from British rule as Rhodesia. After a prolonged civil war, full independence and majority rule were negotiated in 1980.

## Language

The Shona language is also called Shona and is one of the most important of the Bantu languages. It is spoken not only by the Shona but also, as a second language, by many other people in Southern Africa. Many Shona also speak English – a legacy of colonialism.

## Ways of life

**AGRICULTURE** The majority of the Shona people earn their living from agriculture. The staple food crop is corn and other cereal crops grown include wheat, millet, sorghum, and barley. Other important food crops include vegetables, fruit, cassava, and soybeans. Sugar, cotton,

**Nyatsimba Mutota**
Mutota was the founder of the Mwene Mutapa dynasty and ruled from c. 1440 to c. 1450. During this period, he abandoned Great Zimbabwe and took the capital north to the Zambezi River, from where the expansion of Shona territory and influence continued.

**Birds of God**
Made from soapstone, these strange, stylized bird figures with animal-like legs were found at Great Zimbabwe. They are thought to be symbolic of long-dead Shona chiefs who represented a link between the heavens and the Earth. Some people doubt they are birds, but prefer to think of them as forgotten mythological beasts.

© DIAGRAM

73

**Shona headrest**
Dating from the late nineteenth or early twentieth century, the design of this wooden headrest combines concentric circles and triangles – motifs that are said to be a typically Shona. Headrests were once used solely by mature men, who until the end of the nineteenth century commonly wore their hair in elaborate styles. Today, few headrests are used, though some diviners use them as symbolic links with the spirit world.

**Great Zimbabwe: the outer wall**
This is the outer wall of Great Zimbabwe, the largest of the Shona *zimbabwes* (stone houses). The function of its meandering stone walls was largely symbolic – to separate ordinary citizens from nobility.

and tobacco are the main cash crops. The Shona also raise cattle, goats, sheep, pigs, and poultry.

During the colonial period and the following era of white rule, the most fertile farming land in present-day Zimbabwe was taken by white settlers. As a result, many Shona lost their land. Even today, despite official land resettlement schemes, the Shona suffer the legacy of these policies. Land shortages combined with recurring *drought* (inadequate rainfall) mean that few are able to support themselves by agriculture alone. Instead, they have to supplement their income by working in nearby towns.

**INDUSTRY** In Zimbabwe, many Shona work in mining where over forty different minerals are exploited. Gold is the most important mineral and has been mined by the Shona for many hundreds of years. Other important minerals mined are nickel, coal, copper, and iron.

## Social structure

Before colonialism, Shona society was organized into chiefdoms, each led by a hereditary chief. This man would be responsible for land distribution and would judge disputes. Historical records report that most societies were basically egalitarian and chiefs were not markedly more wealthy than their subjects. The authority of the chiefs is still recognized, but they no longer have any real political power. Instead, they now perform the more socially oriented function of maintaining and preserving Shona culture and values.

**MARRIAGE** Most Shona have only one marriage partner. An important part of marriage arrangements is the *bridewealth,* which is given by the groom to the bride's family. Previously this sum was in cattle but it is now more likely to be cash. Alternatively, some sort of service can be provided instead of cash. The families of well-educated girls normally demand a higher amount. If a couple divorces, a negotiable proportion of the original bridewealth has to be repaid.

## Culture and religion

**RELIGION** With colonialism came Christian missionaries. Although they made little headway at first, over a quarter of all Shona are Christians today. The majority are members of independent churches established, attended, and controlled largely by Africans, not by Europeans. Also, the Shona religion is still widely followed and remains a vital force in Shona society.

The Shona religion involves the recognition of a supreme god, referred to in historical documents as *Murungu* but more commonly called *Mwari* today. A major part of the Shona religion involves ancestral spirit cults. The spirit of an ordinary person is known as a *mudzimo* while that of someone more influential as *mhondoro.* Mhondoro spirits provide the link between mortals and Mwari. When they possess a medium they can intercede with Mwari on behalf of the people, on ethical as well as practical matters such as predicting rainfall. Harmful spirits called *ngozi* are thought to cause evil and they can be the spirits of people who were murdered. *N'anga* are religious and medical practitioners who both heal illnesses with herbs and diagnose evil forces at work through various means of *divination.*

The incoming religion of Christianity and the already present Shona religion have each altered in response to the presence of the other. Many of the independent churches incorporate so-called "traditional" beliefs about healing into their form of Christianity, so that the Holy Spirit is believed to heal through possession; in turn, the Shona religion has developed a "traditional" creation story that was not in existence before colonialism.

**Shona pottery** *(above)* This Shona pot, from Zambia, was made in the 1960s. From early times, pottery has been an important part of Shona culture. In the kitchen buildings of many ancient *zimbabwes* (stone houses), stepped platforms can be seen on which women displayed their pots. The pots were highly valued and their display celebrated the household, marriage, and the woman's central role in these institutions. Even today, such platforms can be found in old-fashioned Shona homes.

**Soapstone figurine**
This soapstone figurine was found at Great Zimbabwe. It has a pointed end that could have been used to stand it upright in a stone or clay base. Little is known of its use, though it may have had a religious role.

© DIAGRAM

# The abandoned civilization of Great Zimbabwe

In the southeast of Zimbabwe, not far from the town of Masvingo, a small granite hill rises steeply to a height of about 350 ft (100 m) above the surrounding plains. At the top and to the south of the hill, stand the massive granite walls that are the remains of the ancient Shona civilization of Great Zimbabwe.

Great Zimbabwe was the largest of about 200 similar zimbabwes (literally, stone houses) – the palaces of Shona kings and chiefs – scattered throughout Zimbabwe and neighboring parts of Mozambique and South Africa. The Shona first began to construct these impressive dry-wall stone enclosures – built without mortar – in the late 1100s. This building system was perfected in the building of the Great Zimbabwe palace, which reached a peak in the 1300s and 1400s. The quality of the stonework at the site is so impressive that for many years some people believed that no indigenous African people could possibly have been the builders.

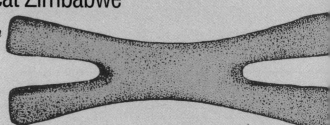

**Ingot** (above)
The currency of Great Zimbabwe consisted of copper ingots (metal bars). Soapstone molds for making these ingots have been found at Great Zimbabwe and the ingots themselves have turned up as far away as China.

**The conical tower** (right)
This huge conical tower inside the Great Zimbabwe complex is regarded as the greatest architectural and technical achievement of the early Shona people. Originally thought to be hollow inside, it is now believed to be solid. It is 35 ft (10 m) high and 17 ft (5 m) across at the base.

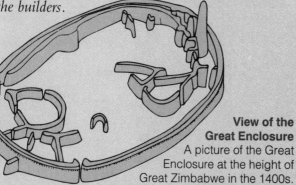

**View of the Great Enclosure**
A picture of the Great Enclosure at the height of Great Zimbabwe in the 1400s.

## Symbol of wealth

For about four hundred years, from the twelfth to the sixteenth centuries, the site of Great Zimbabwe – and the city that grew up around it – was the political, religious, and commercial center of a prosperous Shona civilization.

The great wealth of the Shona people, which enabled them to build Great Zimbabwe, was based on agriculture, mining, and trade. They grew crops;

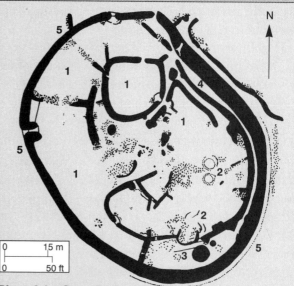

**Plan of the Great Enclosure**
The Great Enclosure – the finest of the Shona dry-wall *zimbabwes* (stone houses) – is part of the main Great Zimbabwe site, which also includes the Western and Eastern enclosures. Work on the site was begun in the late 1100s and continued for over three hundred years. All the walls were built without mortar, the earlier parts being undressed stone. Later parts feature dressed stone and beautiful, chevron-patterned friezes.

### Key
1 Enclosure    3 Conical tower    5 Outer wall
2 Stone platform    4 Parallel passage

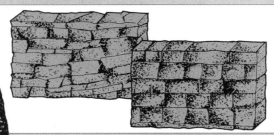

**Stonework**
Shown here are two examples of stonework from Zimbabwe. One *(far left)* is from earlier buildings and the other is a later example. Technical improvements can be seen in the quality of the stonework.

*To get the stones with which they built the walls, the Shona masons used a technique probably first developed by their miners. They built fires around boulders or outcrops of granite to heat them up, then doused the rocks with cold water. This sudden cooling split them into slabs 3 to 7 in. (7.5–17 cm) thick. These slabs were then dragged on sledges to the construction site, where they were cut into small blocks with stone hammers and iron chisels.*

### Abandonment and plunder
*Great Zimbabwe lost its importance as a political center in the middle of the fifteenth century, when the Shona kings abandoned the site and moved their capital north to the area around the Zambezi River; it continued only as a religious and ceremonial site. The site was completely abandoned in the 1830s, when most of its inhabitants were driven out or taken prisoner by Nguni peoples fleeing from the Zulu Mfecane/Difaqane.*

*The Nguni ignored, or did not find, most of the treasures of Great Zimbabwe. In the late nineteenth century, the ruins were discovered by Europeans and the buried riches were plundered by treasure hunters. Nearly all of the priceless gold artifacts were melted down and so lost forever.*

*raised cattle; mined and worked iron, copper, and gold; and controlled the trade routes between the interior of Africa and the Arab/Swahili ports on the coast of what is now Mozambique. Through these coastal ports they exported gold, copper, and ivory and imported silks and porcelain from China; glass beads from Indonesia, India, and Europe; and faience (expensive, highly-colored glazed pottery) from Persia (modern Iran).*

### Walls and buildings
*The massive stone walls of Great Zimbabwe form enclosures that contained mud-walled and thatched-roofed circular buildings, some up to 30 ft (9 m) or more in diameter. The largest buildings were often divided internally into separate rooms and had roofs about 20 ft (6 m) high. The stone walls themselves are up to 30 ft (9 m) high and about 16 ft (5 m) thick at the base; their foundations were built in carefully prepared and leveled trenches.*

**Clay ox**
This clay model of an ox dates from the eleventh century and was found in the Western Enclosure of Great Zimbabwe.

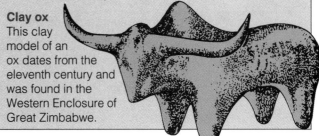

# Sotho

The Sotho (or Basotho) are one of the principal Bantu-speaking peoples of Southern Africa. There are about 2.5 million Northern Sotho who live in northern and eastern Transvaal, a province of South Africa. A further two million Southern Sotho live in the Orange Free State – also part of South Africa – and in the independent Kingdom of Lesotho.

## History

The Bantu-speaking ancestors of the Sotho originated in present-day eastern Nigeria. There, over 2,000 years ago, they developed a way of life based on farming and ironworking. These people gradually spread southward and by about 1000 they had settled on the Highveld – the high arid plains to the west of the Drakensberg Mountains – and in the valleys of the Orange, Vaal, and Tugela rivers. They slowly absorbed the existing population, the Khoisan, adopting many aspects of their culture including elements of their languages and many of their musical instruments. By about 1400, the Sotho had established their main *clans* (several families who share the same ancestor or ancestors). Each clan adopted an animal, such as a wildcat, porcupine, or a

### Sotho timeline

| | |
|---|---|
| **200s** | Bantu-speaking peoples begin to arrive in Southern Africa |
| **by 1400** | Emergence of Sotho *clans* |
| **1600s– 1800s** | Bapedi Empire of Northern Sotho Pedi clan |
| **1819– 1839** | *Mfecane/Difaqane*: period of mass migrations and wars: Boers colonize Northern Sotho |
| **1824** | Moshoeshoe founds Basuto |
| **1851– 1852** | Sotho-British wars I and II: British withdraw from Sotho land |
| **1855** | Height of Basuto Kingdom |
| **1858** | Basuto at war with Boers |
| **1860– 1867** | Sotho and Venda drive Boers south of Olifants River |
| **1865– 1868** | Basuto at war with Boers; Basuto made a British colony |
| **1880– 1881** | "Gun War": Sotho rebel when British try to disarm them |
| **1907** | Nationalist movements emerge; Progressive Association formed |
| **1913** | South African Sotho restricted to inadequate "native reserves" |
| **1966** | Basuto independent as Lesotho (a constitutional monarchy) |
| **1979** | King bans opposition parties |
| **1986** | South Africa blockades Lesotho after king refuses to expel African National Congress (ANC) activists; military coup (probably South African-backed) follows and 60 ANC members are expelled |
| **1991** | Military coup in Lesotho |
| **1993** | Elections end military rule |
| **1995** | Letsie III abdicates and Moshoeshoe II becomes king |
| **1996** | Death of Moshoeshoe II |

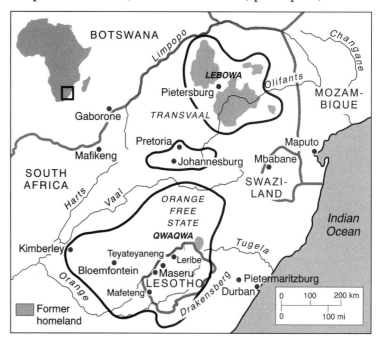

crocodile as its symbol, or totem. Groups of these clans eventually came together to form the three major divisions of the Sotho people: the Northern Sotho, the Southern Sotho, and the Tswana (or Western Sotho). The Tswana are now generally viewed as a separate ethnic group from the other Sotho peoples.

During the seventeenth century, the Pedi group of clans became dominant among the Northern Sotho and established the Bapedi Empire, which lasted for over 200 years. During the same period, the Southern Sotho were living in an age of relative peace and prosperity. This was to last until the 1820s, when the lives of all the Sotho peoples were disrupted by the *Mfecane/Difaqane* – two decades of invasion, warfare, and famine triggered by the Zulu upheavals east of the Drakensberg Mountains. After the Mfecane, the Bapedi lands were taken over by Afrikaners, or Boers. This region (now Transvaal) eventually became part of South Africa. The introduction of *apartheid* (the racist doctrine of "separate development") in 1948 made the Northern Sotho third-class citizens in their own land. In 1959, the South African government attempted to divide the black population from the whites by creating *homelands* or *Bantustans* in which black people were forced to live. The Northern Sotho were allocated a number of separate regions within Transvaal, collectively known as the Lebowa homeland.

In the south, the only people to resist the Mfecane were some members of the Kwena (Crocodile) clan, led by their chief Moshoeshoe I, who was able to unify the Southern Sotho clans and establish the Basuto Kingdom. After losing about two-thirds of his country's arable land to the Afrikaners' newly-formed Orange Free State, Moshoeshoe requested British protection. In 1868, the country became the British *protectorate* of Basutoland, which remained a British colony until it gained independence in 1966 as Lesotho.

**RECENT EVENTS** The abolition of apartheid laws, in 1991, has given all South African citizens equal rights.

**Basotho ponies**
The Basotho (or Basuto) pony, one of the world's toughest breeds, has its origins in Cape horses brought to Lesotho by Moshoeshoe in 1828. Tracks passable by four-wheel drive vehicles have only recently been provided in the mountain areas of Lesotho, so the horse is still an important form of transport in these regions. Also, pony-trekking is a popular pastime for tourists.

**Moshoeshoe I**
In the 1820s, Moshoeshoe, the son of a Sotho chief, founded a wealthy mountain kingdom – the Basuto (Lesotho) Kingdom – that was protected from the Zulu *Mfecane/Difaqane.*

© DIAGRAM

79

**Initiation costume**
As part of an initiation ritual, this girl is wearing a straw mask that covers her face. Historically, Sotho boys and girls both underwent initiation rites at special lodges or schools to mark their transition to adulthood; the boys in the winter months and the girls in summer. Some Sotho boys and girls still undergo initiation.

**Sotho beadwork**
This unusual doll is a fine example of Sotho beadwork. It has been made using wood, glass beads, and a metal button.

In 1994, the Land Rights Bill – designed to help people in South Africa regain land lost since 1913 because of unjust laws – was introduced.

In Lesotho in 1994, King Letsie III and some sections of the military tried to take power, unsuccessfully, from the democratically-elected government, which was led by Dr Ntsu Mokhehle. King Letsie abdicated and the former king – Letsie's father, Moshoeshoe II – was restored to the throne in 1995. After Moshoeshoe's death in 1996, however, Letsie became king again.

## Language

Northern Sotho (or Sesotho sa Leboa) is spoken in South Africa and the closely-related Sesotho in Lesotho.

## Ways of life

The Sotho have a long history of agriculture. Until the late nineteenth century, they accumulated wealth in the form of cattle and exported grain to other parts of Southern Africa. But since then, a large proportion of the able-bodied men have become migrant laborers who leave their homes to work in the gold, diamond, and coal mines and other industries of South Africa. In the rural areas, the women they leave behind have to raise the children and tend the farms, often single-handed. They raise cattle, sheep, goats, and pigs; corn, sorghum, wheat, and vegetables are grown, but farming is hampered by overgrazing and soil erosion. Most depend on the money sent back to them by the men.

Many people have left the land to live in the lowland towns that serve as temporary homes for migrant workers on their way to and from the mining and industrial areas of South Africa. Typical of these "camp towns" are those along the northwestern and western borders of Lesotho, including Teyateyaneng, Leribe, Mafeteng, and the capital, Maseru.

## Social structure

SOCIAL STRUCTURE The main social levels of Sotho society are clan-groups, individual clans, *lineages*, and families. The members of each clan share a common name referring to the originator or founding father of that clan. Within each clan are lineages (extended families descended from a common ancestor). Several lineages comprise a clan. The lineages are divided into families and groups of families live together in villages.

**POLITICAL STRUCTURE** The Sotho are now ruled by democratic central government structures and so the traditional hierarchy of chiefs has lost much of its power, but it still survives as a social force. At the top of the hierarchy is the paramount chief or king, and below him are the chiefs, subchiefs, and headmen. Chiefs exercise their powers in consultation with all the adult males of their areas, and reach their decisions at *pitsos* (public meetings) held in their *kgotlas* (courts or meeting places).

## Culture and religion

**RELIGION** The majority of Sotho are now Christians, but many still follow the Sotho religion, which they share with the Tswana. The souls of the dead are believed to have the power to influence the lives of the living and the Sotho make offerings to these *badimo* to thank them for their help or to ask them for assistance.

The Sotho also have professional alternative medical practitioners who employ a wide range of herbal medicines and rituals to cure diseases, bring good luck and fertility, and protect people from misfortune. In South Africa, the health authorities have come to recognize the value of these health workers. Instead of trying to obliterate such practices, which were scorned under apartheid, the government has tried to incorporate them into the official health system at the community level. Workshops and courses are provided to give them a wider healthcare education.

**ORAL LITERATURE** The Sotho have a rich culture of poetry, song, dance, and storytelling. This includes *lithoko*, or praise poems; *lifela,* songs describing the life of migrant laborers; and *tumellano,* in which groups of people sing together in harmony.

**Sotho compound**
In the past, most Sotho families would live in a *compound* of linked circular houses with stone or wicker walls and conical thatched roofs. Nowadays, housing is less predictable and different materials and designs are also likely to be used. Unlike in South Africa where *apartheid* policies dictated the housing facilities of the Sotho (which were generally poor), settlements such as this can more often be found in Lesotho.

**Sotho pipe**
Finely carved and made from wood, tobacco pipes like this one were once normally used by both men and women. The quality, style, and size of a pipe indicated the social status of its owner. Pipes were handed down from one generation to the next. © DIAGRAM

# Swazi

The Swazi comprise over ninety percent of the 906,000 inhabitants of Swaziland, an independent kingdom located between South Africa and Mozambique. Many more Swazi live in the neighboring areas of South Africa (largely in the former *homeland* of KaNgwane) and Mozambique.

## History

The Swazi are descended from a group of Bantu-speaking peoples called the Nguni who migrated from present-day eastern Nigeria to what is now Mozambique before the late fifteenth century. Dlamini I was their leader, and his descendants became the Swazi kings. About 1750 Ngwane II, the earliest king commemorated in Swazi ritual, led his people into Swaziland. At this time, both the kingdom and people were known as Ngwane.

**SWAZI KINGDOM** In 1839, Mswati I succeeded to the Ngwane throne at the age of thirteen, so his mother, Thandile, ruled as regent until he came of age in 1845. Thandile set the foundations for the success of Mswati's reign by centralizing the kingdom and introducing *age-regiments* (groups who could be called upon for work or warfare) and establishing royal

### Swazi timeline

| | |
|---|---|
| **200s** | Bantu-speaking peoples begin to arrive in Southern Africa |
| **300s–400s** | Bantu-speakers reach modern Transvaal (South Africa) |
| **c. 1750** | Swazi king, Ngwane II, alive |
| **by 1800** | Ngwane kingdom one of most powerful in region (present-day KwaZulu/Natal in South Africa) |
| **c. 1815–1839** | Reign of King Sobhuza I over Ngwane kingdom |
| **1816** | Ngwane driven north by Ndwandwe kingdom |
| **1819–1839** | *Mfecane/Difaqane*: period of mass migrations and wars |
| **1836–1848** | Great Trek brings Boers into conflict with people inland |
| **1839–1865** | Reign of Mswati I over Ngwane; Swazi kingdom founded |
| **1879** | British and Swazi defeat Pedi |
| **1894** | Swaziland made a British colony (administered by the Boer's Transvaal republic until 1902) |
| **1910** | White-minority ruled Union of South Africa created |
| **1913** | Swazi in South Africa restricted to inadequate "native reserves" |
| **1948** | *Apartheid* begun in South Africa |
| **1968** | Swaziland independent as a semiconstitutional monarchy |
| **1973** | Swazi king dissolves parliament |
| **1978** | New constitution approves king's absolute hold on power |
| **1991** | Apartheid legislation repealed |
| **1994** | First nonracial elections are held in South Africa |
| **1995** | Swazi opposition launches arson and bombing campaign |

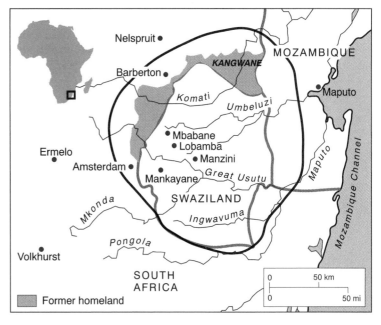

villages around the country to control them. The previous king, Sobhuza I (reigned c. 1815–39), and the powerful Mswati I (reigned 1839–65) extended their territory and effectively forged Swaziland by fusing local peoples and refugees from the Zulu *Mfecane* into a nation powerful enough to resist Zulu pressure. Swazi means "the people of Mswati," and, since the nineteenth century, this name has been given to both the people and the nation previously known as Ngwane.

Toward the Boers, the Swazi kings pursued friendly policies in the later nineteenth century; by granting them concessions, however, the Swazi lost their land, resources, and finally their independence on becoming a British colony, administered by the Boers, in 1894.

**RECENT EVENTS** Swaziland became independent as a constitutional monarchy in 1968. In 1973, Sobhuza II (reigned 1921–82) suspended the constitution, banned political parties, and assumed absolute power. Since then, opposition to the loss of democracy has grown. Several protest movements emerged in the early 1990s but, despite various government inquiries and reports, no real changes have been made. In 1995, some dissatisfied extremists began a campaign of arson and bomb attacks on official targets.

## Language
The Swazi language is Swazi (or Swati or siSwazi).

## Ways of life
**AGRICULTURE** The majority of Swazi are farmers. Over fifty percent of land in Swaziland is owned by the monarchy, managed by local headmen, and granted to small-scale farmers to work. The main food crops grown are corn, sorghum, sweet potatoes, *groundnuts* (peanuts), and beans. Cash crops include, cotton, rice, tobacco, citrus fruits, vegetables, and sugar. Cattle, goats, sheep, and chickens are kept.
**ECONOMY** One-third of all adults work for wages in the private sector of the economy.

**Swazi initiate**
The hairstyle worn by this young Swazi man – shaggy and dyed blond – suggests that he is undergoing initiation into adulthood.

**Founder of the Swazi kingdom**
Shown here with Swazi chiefs in full ceremonial dress is King Mswati I (reigned 1839–65). Skillfully using both warfare and diplomacy, Mswati forged a powerful kingdom at a time when the region was under threat from Boer, British, Portuguese, and Zulu aggressors.

© DIAGRAM

## Swazi dress

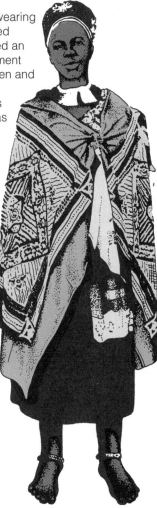

This woman is wearing a brightly-colored body wrap called an *emahiya,* a garment worn by both men and women. Other traditional styles of dress, such as those using animal skins, have largely been replaced by Western-style clothing – except on ceremonial occasions. The emahiya still survives, however, as the design lends itself well to modern methods of mass production.

## Headrest *(below)*

Carved in the distinctive Swazi "grooved" style, this wooden headrest is both functional and aesthetic.

Manufacturing industries employ many people in the processing of agricultural products. Tourism and forestry also provide jobs.

Increasingly, men move away temporarily to find paid work elsewhere in the mines of Swaziland or South Africa. The drift of workers to towns and cities and the growth of large-scale commercial farming of citrus fruits, pineapples, and sugar cane are creating new patterns of living.

**DIVISION OF LABOR** Men generally plow fields and sow seeds while women tend and harvest crops. Because many men work as migrant laborers, however, the division of labor is not strict as the work often has to be done by whoever is available – generally the women.

## Social structure

**SOCIAL ORGANIZATION** The basic social unit is the *indlu* (a husband and wife and their children). Several indlu make up a *umuti.* Each umuti has as its head an *umnumzana,* who is usually male, but with so many men working away from home it is often a woman. The umnumzana settles disputes, allocates land, and organizes workers. The members of an umuti share agricultural tasks. The *clan* (several families who share a common ancestor or ancestors) is the broadest unit.

**MARRIAGE** People belong to the same clan as their father and must marry outside it. Ideally, a man marries a woman from his paternal grandmother's clan. Marriage can be arranged by the parents of the bride and bridegroom but "love" matches are just as common. The groom's family gives the bride's family cattle, cash, or both. Some men have more than one wife but as many Swazi are Christian this is not common.

**POLITICAL STRUCTURE** In Swaziland, the king and his mother have supreme legislative, executive, and judicial powers, which are exercised through a framework of local and political officials and organizations. The king inherits the throne from his father, a member of the powerful Nkosi Dlamini clan. If the last king had many sons by different wives, a family council chooses the new king by taking into account factors such as his mother's rank and his own age and character. Until this crown prince's coming of age – marked by his first marriage – his mother acts as queen regent and she remains influential even after her son is installed as king. The king is given the title *Ngwenyama* (Lion) and his mother is known as *Ndlovukazi* (Lady Elephant).

A prime minister and cabinet ministers, approved by the king, head the government departments, which run the country on a day-to-day basis. Since 1978, the nonparty parliament has been elected indirectly through *tinkhundla* (local authorities based on chieftaincies) – in a system that preserves the king's powers.

## Culture and religion

**RELIGION** Over half of the Swazi are Christians and the Swazi religion is still widely practiced. It involves belief in a creator god, *Mkhulumnqande,* and in ancestors' spirits who can either help or punish their living relatives and so merit respect and appeasement. Many Swazi seek help from religious practitioners who use herbal cures; from *diviners* who use bones, cards, or other devices to diagnose the causes of ailments; and from Christian faith healers. Specialist diviners "smell out" witches who are believed to harm people or their possessions. In Swaziland today, most of these practitioners are officially registered, belong to trade organizations, and many also have set fees.

**FESTIVALS** Famous Swazi cultural institutions include *sibhaca* dancing and the annual *Umhlanga,* or Reed Dance. Sibhaca dancers are teams of men performing vigorous, rhythmic dances in colorful skirts, with their wrists and ankles decorated with cowtails. Dancing also plays a part in the *Incwala,* or First Fruits Festival, a three-week-long period when king and nation reaffirm their relationship. This festival was introduced by Queen Regent Thandile in the nineteenth century to unify the kingdom and raise the king's standing.

**Umhlanga**
Dressed as Swazi warriors, these men are ritually paying court to girls as part of the *Umhlanga,* or Reed Dance. Each September in Swaziland, unmarried girls perform the Umhlanga to pay homage to the queen mother. Wearing necklaces, bead skirts, bracelets, and anklets they perform a dance as they bring reeds from different parts of the country to raise symbolic screens around the queen mother's cattle enclosure.

© DIAGRAM

85

# Tswana

The Tswana (or Batswana or Western Sotho) are one of the principal Bantu-speaking peoples of Southern Africa. The Tswana number about three million and live in a region stretching southeast from the Okavango Swamps to the Limpopo River, and southwest from there to the Kuruman River area. This region includes eastern and northwestern Botswana, and the former Tswana *homeland* of Bophuthatswana, which consisted of a number of separate blocks of territory in South Africa.

## History

The Tswana are descended from Bantu-speaking peoples who migrated southward from present-day eastern Nigeria. They reached the eastern part of their present lands some time between 300 and 400. From there, groups spread slowly westward over the following two centuries and set up new territories and settlements. The Tswana originally emerged as a separate group from within the Sotho group of people sometime before the 1400s. Over many years, groups of Sotho *clans* (several families linked by a common

**Tswana timeline**

| | |
|---|---|
| 200s | Bantu-speaking peoples begin to arrive in Southern Africa |
| 300s–400s | Bantu-speakers reach present-day Transvaal (South Africa) |
| 650–1300 | "Toutswe tradition" in Botswana: large, cattle-owning communities |
| by 1400 | Tswana emerge from Sotho |
| 1801 | First contact with Europeans |
| 1816 | First Christian mission |
| 1819–1839 | *Mfecane/Difaqane*: period of mass migrations and wars |
| 1836–1848 | Great Trek brings Boers into conflict with people inland |
| 1884–1885 | Bechuanaland, British colony, established over Tswana |
| 1910 | Boers and British form white-ruled Union of South Africa |
| 1913 | Tswana in South Africa restricted to "native reserves" |
| 1948 | *Apartheid* officially begins in South Africa |
| 1966 | Bechuanaland independent as Botswana; Tswana leader Seretse Khama is president |
| 1970 | Bophuthatswana, Tswana *homeland*, created by South African government; many Tswana forcibly relocated to this homeland in following years |
| 1980 | Death of Seretse Khama |
| 1991 | Apartheid legislation repealed |
| 1992 | Botswana government in corruption scandal |
| 1994 | First nonracial elections are held in South Africa |
| 1996 | South Africa adopts new constitution |

ancestor or ancestors) came together to form the three major divisions of the Sotho people: the Northern Sotho, the Southern Sotho, and the Tswana (or Western Sotho) – who are now often viewed as a separate group.

The first half of the nineteenth century was a period of turmoil for the Tswana. They had to endure a series of civil wars followed by the *Mfecane/Difaqane* – a period of devastating invasions by neighboring peoples fleeing the Zulu expansion. The Tswana's first contact with Europeans came in 1801, when a small group of explorers reached the southernmost Tswana settlements. These events were followed by occupation and rule by the Afrikaners, or Boers, and the British under whom Tswana lands were divided between South Africa and the British *protectorate* (colony) of Bechuanaland, which became independent in 1966 as Botswana. The country's first president, from 1966 until his death in 1980, was Sir Seretse Khama.

In South Africa, the Tswana were reduced to third-class status by the government's policy of *apartheid* ("separate development") and were required to live in the Bophuthatswana homeland, but allowed to work as migrant laborers elsewhere in South Africa.

**RECENT EVENTS** The Tswana in South Africa have benefited from the abolition of the apartheid laws in the early 1990s, which has given all South Africans equal rights. In Botswana, Sir Ketumile Masire was re-elected as president for a third five-year term in 1994.

## Language
The Tswana language is called Setswana.

## Ways of life
**SETTLEMENTS** Tswana villages can be very large with populations of up to 25,000 people. A typical Tswana *compound* is built in a large yard, usually enclosed by a fence or hedge and containing a garden area plus one or more large trees, for shade. Within the yard, two or more houses providing dwelling and storage space for the family stand in or next to the *lolwapa,* a low-walled courtyard that is the heart of the compound.

**Tswana architecture**
In the past, most Tswana houses were circular, with mud or stone walls and a thatched roof supported on rafters. Today, many Tswana houses are rectangular, however, and made of brick. In fact, a great diversity of housing styles is reflected by modern Tswana homes.

© DIAGRAM

87

**Beer brewing**
This Tswana woman is brewing beer, a profitable cottage industry (largely performed at home using nonmechanized means of production) in Botswana and South Africa.

**AGRICULTURE** As well as its compound, each Tswana family has houses on its farming and cattle-grazing lands, which may be some distance from the village. During the farming season, from November to June, most people in the villages leave for these outlying areas to plow their land, plant and harvest crops, and tend their cattle, goats, and sheep. In Botswana, cattle make up eighty-five percent of total agricultural output and meat products are a major export.

**INDUSTRY** Away from the land, many Tswana men have found work in the mines and industries of South Africa, or in the rapidly-expanding mining industries of Botswana and Zimbabwe.

**DIVISION OF LABOR** The farming work and other tasks are divided between men, women, and children. The men herd and milk the livestock, do the heavier building work, and hunt wild game. They also help with the plowing, but that is often left to the women. The women also tend and harvest the crops – which include sorghum, corn, millet, vegetables, and fruit – and do the cooking and other household jobs. With many men working away from home as migrant laborers, however, it increasingly falls to the women to perform most agricultural work. The children usually help by collecting water and firewood.

**Tswana village** *(right)*
In this plan of a Tswana village in Botswana, a mixture of modern and old-fashioned influences can be seen. Alongside a school, clinic, shops, and restaurants are *compounds* arranged in crescent shapes: according to Tswana custom, male relatives live in neighboring compounds arranged in a crescent shape around the family *kgotla* (meeting place). The main village kgotla is headed by the chief. In modern-day Botswana, chiefs are now elected and paid a salary. Although they have lost much of their power, chiefs are still seen as leaders and deal with many local disputes at the village kgotla.

## Social structure

**AGE-REGIMENTS** In the past, everyone joined an *age-regiment* after initiation into adulthood. These provided a pool of labor for large-scale activities such as rounding up cattle or building compounds and, in the case of the men, they also comprised the army when needed. During the colonial era, many male age-regiments fought for the British army abroad while others were forced to provide labor for tasks such as building roads. In the modern era, the tasks that an age-regiment can be called on to perform are defined in law. Also, every Tswana is no longer a member of an age-regiment. The role of these institutions has largely been replaced by the existence of social clubs, voluntary associations, churches, and other groups that cross divisions based on ethnicity, age, and class.

**MARRIAGE** Although marriages between cousins are encouraged in Tswana society – as they help to keep wealth and property within family groups and strengthen the bonds of kinship between them – most marriages are between people from different family groups. A man may have more than one wife and marriages are usually arranged by the family group or relatives of the bride and groom.

## Culture and religion

**RELIGION** The first Christian missionaries arrived in Tswana lands in 1816. Most Tswana are now Christians, yet their own religion, based on ancestor reverence, still survives and is widely followed. Like Christianity, it is based on the belief that people have immortal souls and that the world was created by a supreme being, called *Molimo.* The Tswana believe that the souls of the dead have the power to influence the lives of the living and make offerings to them to thank them for their help or to ask them for assistance. They also have an enduring belief in the power of magic and its practitioners.

The Tswana used to perform rainmaking ceremonies at the beginning of the farming season. Although these ceremonies have fallen into disuse, many Christian churches now hold prayer days for rain.

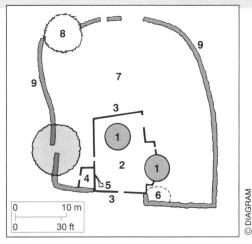

© DIAGRAM

**Tswana compound**
The layout of a typical Tswana *compound.* The main yard is surrounded by a hedge and incorporates a cattle enclosure. The walled inner courtyard, the *lolwapa,* contains one house and has another opening onto it.

| | | |
|---|---|---|
| **1** House | **4** Kitchen | **7** Garden area |
| **2** Lolwapa | **5** Hearth | **8** Kraal |
| **3** Walls | **6** Rubbish area | **9** Outer hedge |

**Tswana warriors**
Pictured in the nineteenth century (a time of great turmoil for the Tswana), the Tswana warrior in front is carrying a distinctively-shaped shield.

# Venda

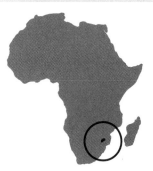

T he Venda (or Vhavenda: "the People of Venda") live in the province of Transvaal in northeastern South Africa just south of the border with Zimbabwe. Their region is also known as Venda. The Venda comprise more than 520,000 people of various subgroups (Vhasenzi, Vhalemba, Vhatavhatsindi, and Vhangona, for example). Each subgroup has its own customs and further subdivisions, yet most share the same language and culture that distinguishes them from Southern Africa's other Bantu-speaking peoples.

## History

The Venda migrated from East Africa's great lakes region to the north in several waves. The first arrivals, the Vhangona, reached the Limpopo River by the 1100s. A Venda group led by Thoho ya Ndou was the first to cross the Limpopo and enter the northern region of present-day Transvaal, most likely in the 1600s. Large, powerful bows probably gave the Venda a military edge over the previous inhabitants and for a time they controlled much of eastern Southern Africa. Rivalries between Thoho ya Ndou's descendants lost the Venda their supremacy, however, and kept them divided into a number of chiefdoms. During a Swazi invasion in 1839, the decentralized structure of the state and its mountain

### Venda timeline

| | |
|---|---|
| **by 1100s** | First Venda group, Vhangona, reach north of Limpopo River after migrating from great lakes region of East Africa |
| **1600s** | Venda led by Thoho ya Ndou cross Limpopo and arrive in present-day Transvaal |
| **1819–1839** | *Mfecane/Difaqane*: period of mass migrations and wars |
| **1836–1848** | Great Trek brings Boers into conflict with people inland |
| **1840s** | Boer republic of Soutpansberg established on Venda lands |
| **1858–1864** | Soutpansberg incorporated into Boer's Transvaal republic |
| **1860–1867** | Venda drive Boers out of their lands north of Olifants River |
| **1898** | Venda conquered by Transvaal |
| **1910** | British Natal and Cape colonies and Boer's Orange Free State and Transvaal republics unite to form the white-minority ruled Union of South Africa |
| **1913** | Venda restricted to inadequate "native reserves" |
| **1948** | *Apartheid* officially begins |
| **1973** | Venda *homeland* created from "native reserves" |
| **1979** | Venda homeland given artificial "independence," which is not recognized outside of South Africa |
| **1991** | Apartheid legislation repealed |
| **1994** | First nonracial elections won by African National Congress (ANC) led by Nelson Mandela. Homelands are reabsorbed |
| **1996** | New constitution is adopted |

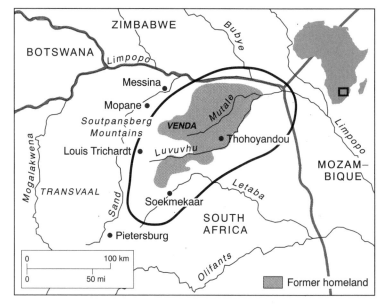

refuges helped save the Venda from being wiped out. Later that century, though, they suffered from famines and wars of succession.

In the 1840s, Afrikaners established the Soutpansberg republic in Venda. At first it was basically a hunting settlement, employing Venda men to hunt for ivory but the Boers (Afrikaner farmers) established a large army to carry out slave-raids on Venda villages. The Venda rose in rebellion and by 1867 had ousted all the white settlers from their land. Gradually, however, Boer commandos isolated and defeated the Venda chiefdoms one by one. An onslaught in 1898 finally drove the remaining Venda north of the Limpopo River and the Venda lands were incorporated into the Boers' South African Republic (later, Transvaal).

**RECENT EVENTS** In 1910, the British colonies and the Boer republics were united as the white-minority ruled Union of South Africa. Racist policies increasingly began to be used to oppress the Venda, along with all other black South Africans, and the Venda were restricted to three small "native reserves." After the 1948 election, *apartheid* (the racist doctrine of "separate development") came into being  In 1973, the government turned the reserves into a "self-governing" *homeland*, which was given "independence" in 1979. This independence was fictional, however, and never recognized outside of South Africa. After the end of white-minority rule in 1994, South Africa reabsorbed the homelands.

## Language

The Venda language is Luvenda (or Tshivenda).

## Ways of life

**AGRICULTURE** Most Venda inhabit the well-watered land between the Soutpansberg Mountains and the Letaba River to the southeast. A large tract north of the mountains is drier, more subject to *drought*, less fertile, and more sparsely peopled. The majority of the Venda live in sizable farming villages of stone or thatched homes surrounded by fences or walls and sited on hillsides. The region allocated to the Venda by the apartheid system was insufficient for the population and

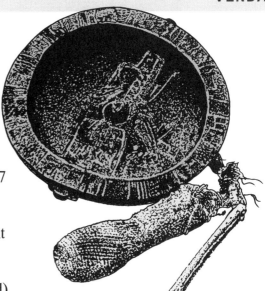

**Divining bowl**
This *ndilo* (divining bowl) is made from wood, bone, and fiber and dates from the 1800s. It was used at the courts of Venda chiefs to identify witches. The images carved on the rim represent different Venda subgroups. If any of these was touched by a seed floating in the bowl, then it would indicate the presence of a witch in that group.

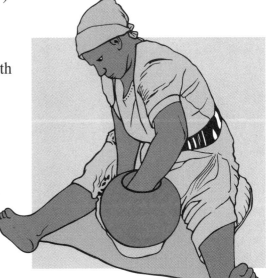

**Venda potter**
This Venda woman is fashioning a pot. Pieces of the pods of certain plants are used to shape and smooth the pots, which are then usually fired in a pit.

© DIAGRAM

**Girl drumming**
Many Venda girls are accomplished drummers. The python dance of the *domba* (female initiation society), for example, is accompanied by drumming performed by girls.

**Matano figures**
Made from clay or wood, *matano* figures are used to illustrate the stories and *milayo* (aphorisms) that are part of the teaching process of girls undergoing initiation. Until recently, mutano figures were kept at the chief's capital for use in the initiation schools. Today, these figures are more likely to be hired each time from the carver. These four figures were carved by Nelson Mukhuba and represent the four stages of a woman's life: childhood; graduation from *domba* (the female initiation society); marriage and motherhood; and old age.

never received adequate investment. Consequently, cropland is in short supply and is shrinking further as the population rises, and soil erosion is a problem. The Venda chiefly grow crops to eat, yet most of their food has to be imported from other parts of South Africa. Dryland food crops include corn, millet, sorghum, and peanuts. On the region's much smaller area of irrigated land, people grow corn, wheat, sweet potatoes, beans, peas, vegetables, and citrus fruits. Cash crops include *sisal* (a fiber crop), tea, coffee, sugar cane, tobacco, and cotton. Nearly nine-tenths of the land is suitable only for grazing. The Venda raise a few cattle and also sheep, goats, and chickens.

**INDUSTRY** Lack of investment in Venda during the apartheid years has meant that the region has poor infrastructure and therefore few large industries. Also, businesses were previously encouraged to set up on the edge of homelands – in order to take advantage of the cheap labor force – but not inside. As a result, more than one in ten of the population commutes to work in mines and factories outside Venda. Nevertheless, there is some forestry and freshwater fish farming within Venda. Mines yield some copper and graphite, and quarries produce sandstone. Various small-scale industries include ceramics, woodcrafts, and sawmilling.

## Social structure

**SOCIAL STRUCTURE** The basic social unit consists of a husband (generally the head of the family), his wife or wives, and their children. Each extended family involves two sets of relationships, based on male and female lines of descent. The male line includes a father, his brothers and sisters, and his and his brothers' children. The female line includes a wife, her brothers and sisters, and her and her sisters' children. This female line is especially important on religious occasions. *Lineages* that share a common ancestor or ancestors are grouped into *clans,* whose members generally do not intermarry.

**POLITICAL STRUCTURE** Historically, large Venda chiefdoms ruled over, or strongly influenced, smaller ones. Within his area, each chief had the role of lawmaking and other powers, but certain officials and relatives played important roles too. A council advised him on royal village affairs such as ceremonies and public works. A private council of influential men advised him on local affairs, including items he planned to bring up at the next meeting of the council – a body that could freely criticize any of the chief's decisions.

Apartheid established a framework of so-called "traditional" chiefs to administer the Venda homeland. These chiefs were at first appointed by the government but provisions were later made for limited voting rights within the Venda homeland. This established a falsely traditional political structure as it was dependent not on Venda culture but the approval of the white-minority South African regime, even after the Venda were given their "independence" in 1979. Since the dismantlement of apartheid, the Venda can vote for representatives to the national government and the homeland government has been abolished.

## Culture and religion

**RELIGION** The majority of Venda are Christians, yet traces of the Venda religion linger. The Venda believe witches are women unaware of their terrible influence, and they try to remove this by "good" magic or detecting the witches and driving them out. The Venda also consult *diviners* who try to foretell the future from the patterns produced by seeds and other ingredients placed in a bowl.

**INITIATION** At puberty, girls enter a vast building and undergo the six-day *vhusha* initiation process. This includes learning the evils of premarital sex and adultery. Later, they attend a school known as the *domba* to learn the duties expected of wives and mothers. The process can last from three months to a year. Its special features include the python dance, which is performed by a chain of chanting girls, each holding the forearms of the girl in front. For boys entering adulthood, *murundu* (a *circumcision* ceremony), has largely replaced older initiation rituals.

**LITERATURE** The Venda have a rich store of songs, poems, riddles, legends, and myths, which have all been passed on by mouth from one generation to the next.

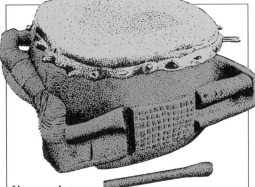

© DIAGRAM

**Ngoma drum**
This *ngoma* drum is only used in the courts of Venda headmen. Ngoma drums are hemispherical and usually elaborately decorated. Legend holds that the first Venda leaders had a ngoma drum, the sound of which alone could defeat their enemies.

**Python dance**
For three months or more, Venda girls undergo a process of initiation called *domba*. A highlight of domba is the python dance, which is regularly performed by the initiates. The dance involves moving close together in a snakelike fashion.

# Xhosa

**Xhosa timeline**

| | |
|---|---|
| **200s** | Bantu-speaking peoples begin to arrive in Southern Africa |
| **300s–400s** | Bantu-speakers reach present-day KwaZulu/Natal |
| **1799–1803** | Cape-Xhosa wars I, II, and III: Xhosa-Boer frontier wars |
| **1811–1812** | Cape-Xhosa War IV: British drive many Xhosa east of Groot-Vis River |
| **1818–1819** | Cape-Xhosa War V: British drive remaining Xhosa east of Groot-Vis River |
| **1819–1839** | *Mfecane/Difaqane*: period of mass migrations and wars |
| **1834–1835** | Cape-Xhosa War VI: British annex Xhosa lands |
| **1836** | British return Xhosa lands |
| **1846–1847** | Cape-Xhosa War VII: British annex Xhosa lands as far east as Great Kei River |
| **1850–1853** | Cape-Xhosa War VIII: Xhosa rebel against British |
| **1856–1857** | Xhosa sacrifice 200,000 cattle in accordance with prophecy |
| **1877–1878** | Cape-Xhosa War IX: final defeat of Xhosa by British |
| **1910** | British and Boers form white-ruled Union of South Africa |
| **1913** | Xhosa restricted to inadequate "native reserves" |
| **1948** | Apartheid in South Africa |
| **after 1959** | Transkei and Ciskei Xhosa *homelands* created |
| **1976** | Transkei "independent" |
| **1981** | Ciskei "independent" |
| **1991** | Apartheid legislation repealed |
| **1994** | First nonracial elections |
| **1996** | New constitution is adopted |

The Xhosa live mostly in rural areas of southeastern South Africa. The overwhelming majority of the black population of Cape Town, Port Elizabeth, and East London are Xhosa and there are also very large Xhosa populations in the Johannesburg area. There are over six million Xhosa, who belong to a diversity of groups, the main ones being the Mpondo, Thembu, Hlubi, Ngqika, and Gcaleka. Together, they are sometimes referred to as Southern Nguni peoples.

## History

The Xhosa are descended from Bantu-speaking peoples from present-day eastern Nigeria who arrived in Southern Africa around the 200s. The Xhosa are one of many ethnic groups who emerged from the Nguni Bantu-speaking peoples. They originally consisted of three main groups: the Mpondo, the Thembu, and the Xhosa. These groups share the same language and hold the belief that their cultures originate from the same source. Over the course of many centuries, internal friction, migration, and contact with the Khoisan-speaking peoples created subdivisions within the original Xhosa groups, which

Former homeland

fragmented into numerous *clans* (extended families or several families who share a common ancestor or ancestors). Sons of chiefs established new chiefdoms of their own and this was the main way in which the Xhosa gradually expanded their territory. Eventually, they occupied an area along the eastern coast that reached roughly from the Groot-Vis River to present-day KwaZulu/Natal and spread inland to the Drakensberg Mountains. The various Xhosa groups remained linked through marriage and political and military alliances.

Between 1779 and 1878 there was a series of nine frontier wars – the Cape-Xhosa wars between the Xhosa and the Boers (Afrikaners) and British of the Cape Colony. In addition, in the early 1800s many Xhosa fled from the northeast of their territory (in what is now KwaZulu/Natal) to escape the armies of the great Zulu leader Shaka. The Xhosa suffered their most traumatic blow in the "cattle-killings" of 1856–7. A young girl called Nongqawuse – said to be possessed by the spirits of the ancestors – had a vision that the white invaders would be swept into the sea, that great Xhosa chiefs would return from the dead, and the land would be filled with cattle and crops. For this to happen, Nongqawuse said, all existing cattle and food supplies must first be destroyed. Coming at a time of great conflict for the Xhosa, many people saw this as a way out of the turmoil. Despite the slaughter of 200,000 cattle, however, the prophecy was not fulfilled and only hunger, death, and poverty resulted. Survivors of this desperate act of resistance were compelled to seek work on the invaders' farms and the Xhosa were finally defeated in 1878.

**RECENT EVENTS** Under *apartheid* (the racist doctrine of "separate development"), the South African government created *homelands* for the country's black population. The Xhosa homelands of Ciskei and Transkei were later declared "independent" by the government, which then withdrew South African citizenship from all Xhosa. After South Africa's first nonracial elections in 1994, Ciskei and Transkei were reabsorbed into South Africa.

**Pipe**
This long pipe has been made using wood, thread, and glass and seed beads and has a metal bowl. Beadwork continues to be an important Xhosa craft though much of the output is produced for sale to tourists.

**Xhosa headdress**
This woman has painted her face with *ocher* (a reddish-brown clay) and wears a headdress of a type often described as "traditional." In fact, fabric headdresses have only been worn since the arrival of mass-produced cloth. Fashion dictates the large size.

© DIAGRAM

## Language

The Xhosa language is Xhosa (or isiXhosa), which is one of the Bantu languages. Along with Zulu, it is one of the most widely spoken South African languages.

## Ways of life

Until most of their land was taken by Europeans, the Xhosa were a cattle-raising people whose herds represented wealth and social stability. Although cattle continues to be important in rural areas, few Xhosa survive purely from the land (which tends to be of poor quality). Instead, most rural Xhosa rely on family members working in the cities to send money home.

Under apartheid, Black Africans were unable to live within city boundaries and instead were confined to government-built *townships,* usually located considerable distances from places of work and with their residency dependent on continuous employment. With the end of apartheid, there are no longer restrictions on where people may live, but living conditions remain fundamentally unchanged. In common with the black urban population as a whole, most Xhosa are employed in manufacturing industries, mining, and domestic service.

## Social structure

POLITICAL STRUCTURE Historically, the Xhosa's allegiance was to their clan, led by an *inkosi* (chief) whose status was gained through his mother. Inkosi were obliged to be hospitable and generous – "inkosi" actually means "thank-you" – and their powers were limited by public opinion and counselors. Within the homelands, so-called "traditional" forms of government were encouraged by the South African government. In fact, they were often falsely so as they had none of the power balances the Xhosa's own system incorporated. The use of ethnicity and "tradition" in this way during apartheid has led many to regard them as inappropriate – President Nelson Mandela (a Thembu), for instance, states that he is not a "tribalist" but a South African. After the homelands

**Xhosa initiate**

This boy's headdress of lamb's wool and feathers physically sets him apart from others and prepares him for his initiation into manhood. Initiation instills in Xhosa boys the values and moral views of their society.

**Snuff box**

Made from clay and hide scrapings mixed with blood, this snuff (powdered tobacco) box has symbolic protective qualities. This distinctive style of snuff container has historically been associated with the Xhosa people.

were reincorporated into South Africa, in 1994, their governments were abolished and replaced by national government structures.

**SOCIAL STRUCTURE** During the course of the early twentieth century, an urban elite developed that became increasingly distanced socially and culturally from the rural Xhosa. The urban Xhosa were commonly called "School" Xhosa and the rural "Red" Xhosa – named for the fashion of using red *ocher* (a yellow or reddish-brown clay) as a body decoration. The conservative Red Xhosa kept Xhosa beliefs and traditions while the School Xhosa adopted new customs and Christianity. Despite considerable changes in rural areas in recent decades and rural-urban migration, these divisions remain, though they are now less marked.

**MARRIAGE** Although the majority of Xhosa are Christians, many still retain certain Xhosa customs concerned with marriage. *Lobola* (or *bridewealth* – gifts given by the groom's family to the bride's family) is still given even by Christians. The function of lobola is to legitimize the marriage and any children born to the couple.

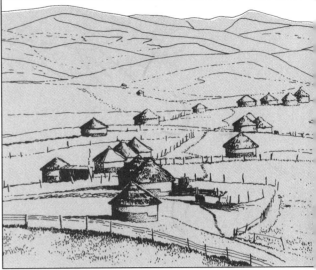

**Xhosa homesteads**
Built on higher ground to keep fertile lowlands free for farming, these Xhosa homesteads have lime-washed walls. Xhosa homes in remote rural areas tend to be strung out along ridges rather than concentrated in villages.

## Culture and religion

**RELIGION** The sufferings that followed the cattle-killings of the mid-nineteenth century caused many Xhosa to lose faith in the power of their own beliefs and turn to Christianity, which is now the Xhosa's main religion.

**LITERATURE** The Xhosa have a long history of literature. Earlier forms are mostly oral and include praise poems, folk tales, and prophecies – many of which have now been written down. This tradition has continued into the present and there are several important Xhosa writers, such as the novelist and playwright John Knox Bokwe and the novelist Sinxo.

**Mother and child**
This Xhosa woman is grinding grain while her baby sleeps on her back.

© DIAGRAM

97

# Zulu

T here are about seven million Zulu, most of whom live in the province of KwaZulu/Natal on the east coast of South Africa. The Zulu emerged from the Nguni group of Bantu-speaking peoples and have close cultural and linguistic links with other Nguni peoples such as the Xhosa and the Swazi. "Zulu" originally referred to the people descended from a man of the same name, but it came to refer to a much broader population after the *Mfecane/Difaqane*.

## History

**MFECANE/DIFAQANE** Before 1816, the Zulu chiefdoms belonged to the Mthethwa kingdom, which was ruled by Dingiswayo. When Dingiswayo died, his Zulu general Shaka took over. With military skill and ruthlessness, Shaka founded the Zulu kingdom and launched the Mfecane – a series of wars and migrations triggered by the rapid expansion of the Zulu nation. This wave of conflict, which lasted from 1819 to 1839, left an estimated five million people dead and made the region vulnerable to takeover by white settlers.

After 1836, the Zulu came into conflict with the growing number of white settlers, first the Afrikaners,

### Zulu timeline

| | |
|---|---|
| 200s | Bantu-speaking peoples begin to arrive in Southern Africa |
| 300s–400s | Bantu-speakers reach present-day Kwazulu/Natal |
| 1787 | Birth of Shaka |
| 1816 | Shaka becomes Zulu leader |
| 1818–1819 | Zulu-Ndwandwe War establishes Zulu supremacy |
| 1819–1839 | *Mfecane/Difaqane*: period of mass migrations and wars |
| 1828 | Shaka assassinated, Dingane succeeds him as Zulu leader |
| 1838 | Zulu defeated by Boers at the Battle of Blood River |
| 1840 | After defeating Dingane, Mpande becomes Zulu leader |
| 1872 | Cetshwayo becomes Zulu king |
| 1879 | British conquer Zulu |
| 1883–1884 | Zulu Civil War after British partition Zululand |
| 1885–1887 | Zululand divided between British Zululand and Transvaal |
| 1910 | White-minority ruled Union of South Africa created |
| 1913 | Zulu restricted to inadequate "native reserves" |
| 1920 | Zululand joined to South Africa |
| 1928 | Inkatha, Zulu nationalist movement, founded |
| 1948 | Apartheid in South Africa |
| 1970s | KwaZulu *homeland* created |
| 1975 | Inkatha reconvened |
| 1980s–1990s | Fighting between Inkatha and ANC supporters |
| 1991 | Apartheid legislation repealed |
| 1994 | First nonracial elections |
| 1996 | Floods in KwaZulu/Natal kill 100 people |

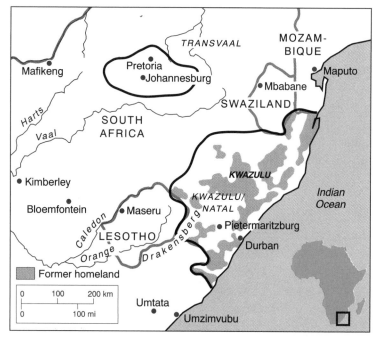

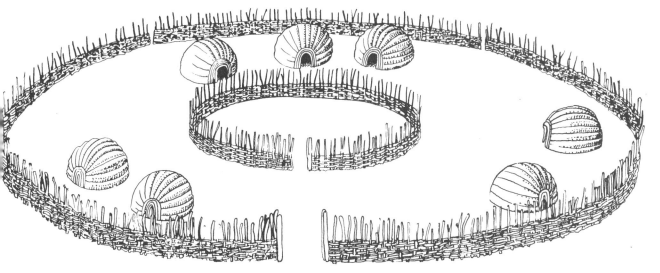

or Boers, and later the British. In 1879 at Isandhlwana, a massive onslaught of Zulu warriors defeated the British, who retaliated later that year and defeated the 40,000-strong Zulu army led by Cetshwayo at Ulundi.

**RECENT EVENTS** In the twentieth century, the Zulu's lives have been dominated by the South African policy of *apartheid* (the racist doctrine of "separate development"), which discriminated against black people in every area of life.

A *homeland*, consisting of only a portion of the original Zululand, was set up for the Zulu in the 1970s. This homeland, called KwaZulu, was in the region of the modern KwaZulu/Natal province of South Africa. Following the end of apartheid in the early 1990s, the Zulu have become a powerful political force. Their Inkatha Freedom Party (IFP), led by Chief Mangosuthu Gatsha Buthelezi, has claimed that the ruling African National Congress (ANC) does not represent their interests, and there have been many violent clashes between Inkatha and ANC supporters.

## Language

The Zulu language is also called Zulu (or isiZulu). Zulu has some 19,000 words and one of the most complex grammars in the world. Many Dutch and English words have been incorporated into Zulu.

**Zulu homestead**
In the past, Zulu homes comprised two concentric fences, with houses in the outer ring and cattle and goods in the inner one. Brick is now preferred and land is in too short supply to build such extensive homesteads. Although a few such villages have been preserved (or created) for tourists to see, they have been compared to human zoos.

**Embedded-wire art**
Barely 3 in. (7.5 cm) in diameter, this snuff (powdered tobacco) container has been crafted using wire embedded into a gourd to form geometric patterns. This technique has transformed the container from a purely practical object into one of great appeal.

© DIAGRAM

99

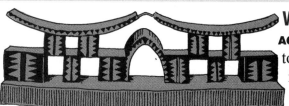

**Zulu headrest**
In the past, Zulu headrests were carved from a single piece of wood. They all had concave strips on top, supported by blocks or feet. Headrests could also be used as stools.

**Figurines**
These two figurines are probably Zulu as they are sporting typically Zulu (if old-fashioned) hairstyles: the man *(right)* a headring and the woman *(left)* a circular tuft of hair.

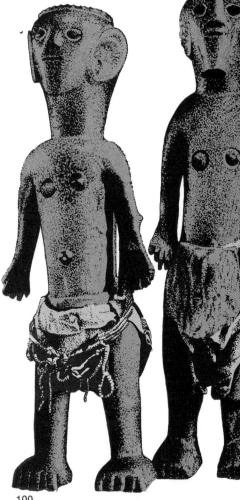

## Ways of life

**AGRICULTURE** Although many men have left Zululand to work as laborers in South Africa's mines and industries, farming is still the backbone of the Zulu economy. The soil is generally poor and suffers from increasing erosion, in spite of this the Zulu are able to grow crops such as millet, corn, sweet potatoes, and vegetables and to raise cattle, sheep, and goats.

**INDUSTRY** Like many other peoples of Southern Africa, the Zulu have a long tradition of metalworking and use their skills to manufacture axes, hoes, spears, and other tools and weapons. Their ceramics are all well-made, simple, and practical and have few decorative additions. Many Zulu are skilled woodworkers and makers of baskets and beadwork artifacts.

## Social structure

The Zulu have a complex social organization that has survived the pressures of modern life relatively intact. It is based on the *imzi,* or homestead, a group of circular thatched houses (or, increasingly, brick-built houses) enclosed by a fence. A number of imzi, spaced at intervals of half a mile to a mile apart, make up a ward, or village. Each imzi is occupied by an elder or imzi head and his extended family, and the other imzi in the ward are usually occupied by related families.

From ward level, the social structure extends upward through district head and clan chief levels to the ultimate head of the Zulu nation, the king. The present king is Zwelethini Goodwill Ka-Cyprian Bhekezulu. The position of the king is one of solely cultural and social importance, however, as the Zulu are governed by the Republic of South Africa.

**MARRIAGE** A man may have more than one wife, but no marriage is considered legitimate until the husband has given *lobola* (or *bridewealth*), usually a gift of cattle, to the bride's family to compensate them for their loss. Marriage between members of the same *clan* (several families who share descent from a common ancestor or ancestors) is discouraged.

# Culture and religion

**RELIGION** Christianity is widespread among the Zulu. There are many independent churches with Zulu clergy as well as Anglican and Catholic churches. Zionist Spirit churches that stress faith healing are also popular. During the apartheid era, people were denied a political voice and this, in part, explains the vibrancy of many churches as they often provided the only forum for people to air their complaints. Christianity coexists with the Zulu religion, which is still widely followed. The Zulu religion is mostly concerned with the reverence of ancestors. Ancestors are believed to directly influence their living descendants so respect must be shown to them. Healing methods as practiced by religious practitioners of the Zulu religion (*diviners*, or *sangomas*, for example) also survive, alongside modern clinics and hospitals, and are used to alleviate diseases thought to arise from defective personal relationships or from supernatural causes. Many of these healers work within the official healthcare system at the local level.

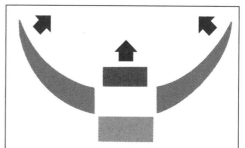

**Battle formation**
As founder of the Zulu kingdom, Shaka devised an ingenious battle formation that helped the Zulus gain military supremacy. It involved four battalions of warriors: the central group would attack the enemy; the side battalions would encircle the enemy; and the last group were the reserves. The warriors would be lined up with their shields touching their neighbors.

**Zulu weapons**
Most of these highly-effective weapons were developed during Shaka's reign and they ensured Zulu supremacy in battle.
**1** A shield made from wood and animal skin.
**2** An iron-bladed throwing spear.
**3** A hardwood knobkerrie (or *iwisa*) sometimes thrown as a weapon.

**Zulu headdresses**
Zulu women are famous for their beadwork, which has become an art-form in itself, as the elaborate headdress on the right shows. Beads were once made from bone, ivory, clay, shells, wood, or iron. Today, however, the tiny colorful beads are mass produced in plastic, allowing women to spend more time on design than bead production.

© DIAGRAM

**1**    **2** **3**

# The Mfecane/Difaqane

In the 1820s, a series of wars and mass migrations in the eastern half of Southern Africa resulted in the loss of countless thousands of lives, the destruction of many kingdoms, and the creation of new ones. This upheaval was the Mfecane, "the crushing," which began in the lands east of the Drakensberg Mountains and spread like bush fire through the neighboring regions. The Mfecane was known as the Difaqane ("the scattering") by the Sotho and Tswana peoples west of the Drakensberg.

## Famine and conflict

The origins of the Mfecane can be traced back to the second half of the eighteenth century, which was a period of relative peace and prosperity in southeast Africa. During this period, rainfall was unusually high, farmers prospered, and the population grew rapidly. But as the nineteenth century began, however, a prolonged drought lasting about ten years brought famine and death to the region.

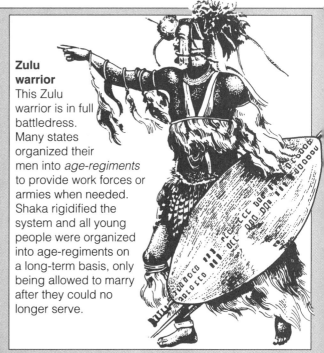

**Zulu warrior**
This Zulu warrior is in full battledress. Many states organized their men into *age-regiments* to provide work forces or armies when needed. Shaka rigidified the system and all young people were organized into age-regiments on a long-term basis, only being allowed to marry after they could no longer serve.

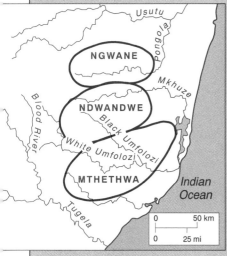

**Three kingdoms**
The most powerful states in the region before the *Mfecane/Difaqane*, were the Ngwane, Ndwandwe, and Mthethwa kingdoms. (At this time, the Zulu state was a chiefdom of the Mthethwa kingdom.) None of these three kingdoms existed after the Mfecane.

In what is now the South African province of KwaZulu/Natal and the southern part of the Kingdom of Swaziland, the most powerful kingdoms were those of three Nguni peoples: the Ndwandwe, their northern neighbors the Ngwane, and the Mthethwa, who lived to their south. As the effects of the famine worsened, these kingdoms competed for farming and grazing land, and small border skirmishes soon erupted into all-out wars.

In 1816 the Ndwandwe, led by Zwide, attacked the Ngwane (ruled by Sobhuza I) and drove them northward from their lands. Two years later, the Ndwandwe attacked and scattered the Mthethwa, occupied much of their land, and killed their leader, Dingiswayo. For a time, the Ndwandwe were the dominant force in the region, but their supremacy was soon to be challenged by a new force that emerged from the ruins of the Mthethwa kingdom.

## The rise of the Zulu

In 1816 Shaka, one of Dingiswayo's military advisors, became leader of the Zulu chiefdom, which was then part of the Mthethwa kingdom. After the defeat of Dingiswayo, Shaka reorganized the Mthethwa chiefdoms and brought them under Zulu control. When they came under renewed attack from Ndwandwe in 1818–19, Shaka's military skills helped them to defeat and destroy the invaders. The Zulu then took control of the Ndwandwe lands and soon controlled most of the land between the

*Drakensberg and the sea. The people displaced by this expansion, such as the Ngwane, Ngoni, and Khumalo fled to the north and to the south, and across the mountains onto the high plains to the west. In doing so, they attacked and dispossessed other neighboring peoples such as the Sotho and the Tswana. This cycle of attack and dispossession continued for nearly twenty years.*

**Zulu hatchet** (right)
Hatchets are among the most interesting of Zulu weapons. Many had brass wire wound around the wooden shaft making them incredibly tough.

**Shaka** (left)
Shaka was born to a Zulu chief but was cast out by his father. He went on, however, to distinguish himself as a soldier of the Mthethwa kingdom. By developing and improving existing warfare techniques to gain military supremacy, he established a powerful Zulu kingdom, which led to the disruption of the *Mfecane*.

**Mfecane/Difaqane**
The map below shows the emerging Zulu kingdom and the migration routes of people forced out of the area. Some of the peoples did not settle for decades while others formed new kingdoms.

**Key**
Zulu kingdom
→ Route of migrating peoples
**SWAZI** New state/kingdom formed by migrating peoples
*(ROZVI)* State/people attacked or conquered by migrating people
Migrating people
1 Sotho              4 Ngoni
2 Khumalo Ndebele    5 Kololo
3 Ngwane

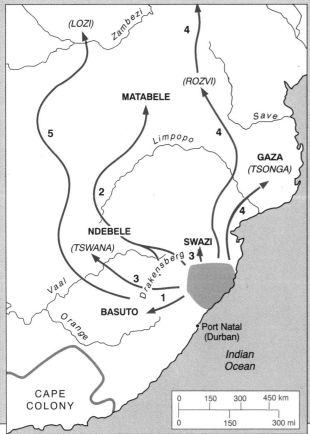

**Consequences of the Mfecane**
*New powerful states such as the Zulu, Sotho, Ndebele, and Swazi kingdoms emerged as a result of the Mfecane. The Swazi kingdom rose from the remnants of the Ngwane kingdom and survived the Mfecane by paying tribute to the Zulu or hiding from Zulu raiding parties in mountain caves. The Sotho kingdom was established by Moshoeshoe, who led his people to safety from the Mfecane in the mountains. Based on a high, flat-topped mountain (Thabia-Bosiu), the Sotho (Basuto) kingdom formed a natural stronghold and attracted refugees, and many local chiefdoms chose to ally themselves with Moshoeshoe for protection. The Ndebele kingdom was established by the Khumalo people – under their leader Mzilikazi – who were forced westward by the Mfecane. Meanwhile, white control over Southern Africa increased as the Afrikaners (Boers) trekking from the Cape took advantage of the situation and colonized the recently-vacated lands.*

© DIAGRAM

# Appendix: Southern African languages

Africans often identify themselves by the language they speak rather than, or in addition to, their ethnic origin or nationality. Language classification in Africa is complex, however; more than 1,000 languages are spoken, most of them "home" languages (native to the continent) and the rest introduced by groups from Europe and Asia who settled in or colonized parts of Africa. Some languages are widely spoken due to historical factors – the use of Shona is widespread, for example, as early Shona civilizations had great influence. Also, the few Muslims learn Arabic because it is the language of the *Koran*, Islam's sacred text. As a result of this diversity, many Southern Africans speak more than one language.

Among the languages introduced to Africa are English, French, Spanish, Portuguese, Italian, Afrikaans, Urdu, Hindi, Gujarati, and Malagasy (the language of Madagascar, which belongs to the Austronesian language family). Afrikaans evolved from seventeenth-century Dutch and has been influenced by African languages and its speakers' experiences in Africa. English and Portuguese are the official languages or the languages of work and commerce in many

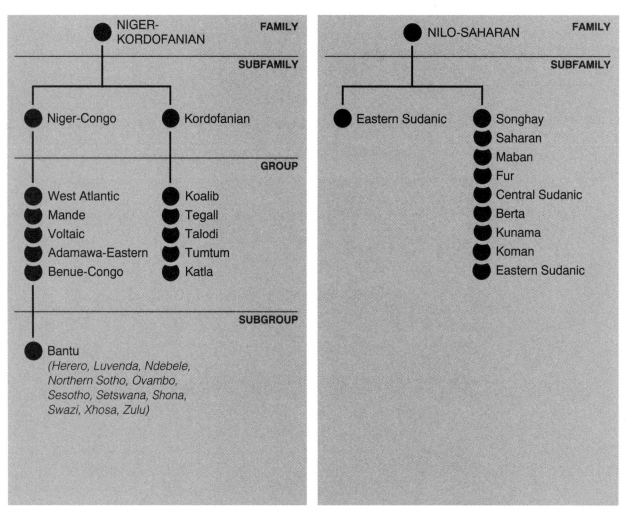

NIGER-KORDOFANIAN — FAMILY

SUBFAMILY
- Niger-Congo
- Kordofanian

GROUP
- West Atlantic
- Mande
- Voltaic
- Adamawa-Eastern
- Benue-Congo
- Koalib
- Tegall
- Talodi
- Tumtum
- Katla

SUBGROUP
- Bantu
  (Herero, Luvenda, Ndebele, Northern Sotho, Ovambo, Sesotho, Setswana, Shona, Swazi, Xhosa, Zulu)

NILO-SAHARAN — FAMILY

SUBFAMILY
- Eastern Sudanic
- Songhay
- Saharan
- Maban
- Fur
- Central Sudanic
- Berta
- Kunama
- Koman
- Eastern Sudanic

Southern African countries – largely a legacy of the colonial era.

The home languages of Africa are divided into four language families: Niger-Kordofanian, Nilo-Saharan, Afroasiatic, and Khoisan. Within these **families** are several **subfamilies**, many of which are also divided into **groups** and again into **subgroups** – only the relevant subgroups have been included. Some groups are themselves languages; other groups or subgroups constitute clusters of individual languages. For example, the Bantu cluster of languages, which is a subgroup of the Benue-Congo group of the Niger-Congo subfamily of the Niger-Kordofanian family, comprises the vast majority of Southern African home languages. Khoisan languages are distinctive for their use of various "click" and popping sounds, many of which have been incorporated into other African – usually Bantu – languages.

Within the diagram below, the languages of the peoples profiled in this volume are printed in *italics*. This appendix can therefore be used to identify the subgroup, group, subfamily, and family of each language and to see how the different languages relate to one another.

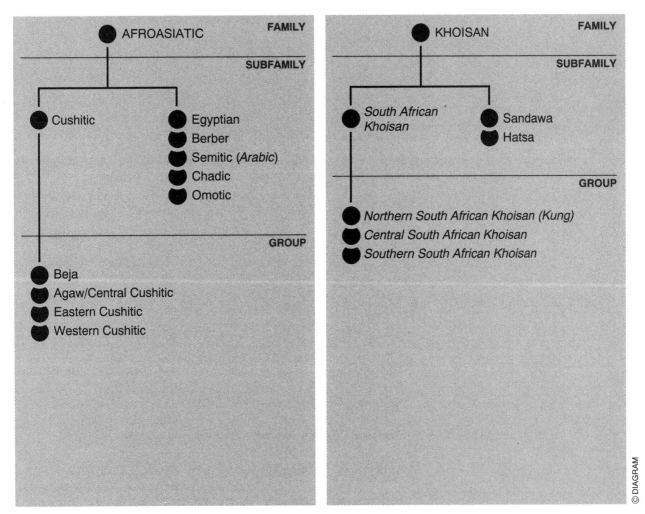

# Glossary

**Bold** words are cross-references to other glossary entries.

**a cappella** Music without instrumental accompaniment.

**age-regiments** A largely historical feature common to many Southern African peoples. Basically, men or women were organized by age into these groups, which were usually used as mobile sources of labor or occasionally provided the army. Different societies structured or organized their age-regiments in various ways. The Zulu age-regiments under Shaka, for instance, were largely concerned with battle and remained together for much longer than in other societies. Age-regiments were an important way of providing social unity.

**aloalo** A carved wooden pole on a Mahafaly tomb.

**amaNdlozi** The revered ancestors of a Ndebele family, who are believed to be spirit guardians.

**apartheid** An Afrikaans word meaning "apartness" or "separateness." It is generally used to refer to the South African government's policy of racial and ethnic segregation and white domination. Officially, apartheid was in effect from 1948 to 1991, though racist policies had been in place before this date and the legacy of apartheid can still be seen today. The government definition of apartheid was "separate development of the races" – a euphemism for oppression.

**badimo** Offerings that Sotho people make to their ancestors to ask for assistance or in gratitude.

**banda** In Herero society, a **lineage** of ancestors that is traced through a person's female relatives.

**Bantustan** An alternative name for a **homeland**.

**Black Consciousness** A movement that emerged in the 1970s and had medical student Steve Biko as one of its leading thinkers. Biko formed the South African Students Organization (SASO), which was based on the principles of Black Consciousness. The movement stressed pride in being black, emphasized black values and culture, and rejected white culture and white liberalism.

**Boeremusiek** Light, danceable Afrikaner country music.

**braaivleis** An Afrikaner barbecue.

**bridewealth** A practice common among African people in which a marriage between a couple is sealed with a gift – often cattle, but it may be cash or other animals – from the groom to the bride's family. It is usually considered to be compensation to the bride's family for loss of a working member or a token of respect. Part of it may be used by the couple to set up home together.

**calabash** A type of gourd whose hollowed-out shell has a wide variety of uses from container to musical instrument. Calabashes often figure in African legends and mythology where the two halves are used, for example, to symbolize the union of Heaven and Earth, Man and Woman, or Land and Sky.

**caste** A rigid class distinction generally based on birth, wealth, and occupation. The Hindu (Indian) caste system consists of four main castes, called varnas. The top varna is occupied by Brahmans (religious leaders and scholars); the next consists of Kshatriyas (rulers, nobles, and warriors); then come the Vaisyas (bankers and other kinds of business people); the lowest varna comprises the Sudras (artisans and laborers). Besides the four varnas there is a fifth category called outcastes, panchamas (fifths), untouchables, or the "Children of God."

**chimurenga** A contemporary African music based on the rhythms of the **mbira**. Created by Thomas Mapfumo, chimurenga – which means "liberation war" – played an important role in the struggle for majority rule in Zimbabwe (then Rhodesia).

**circumcision** A relatively simple, if painful, procedure (removal of all or part of the foreskin) for boys but a much more serious operation (ranging from minor to severe genital mutilation) with long-lasting consequences for girls. This practice is highly controversial, however, and is opposed by many African women.

**clan** A group of people, usually several **lineages**, who claim descent from a common ancestor or ancestors.

**compound** An enclosure containing living quarters. Compound is often used to refer to a group of buildings lived in by members of the same family or extended family. One compound may include several buildings.

**deforestation** The clearing of trees in a forest. Many forests have been cut down to raise much-needed cash. Also, the growth of urban areas has led to the intensification and extensification of agriculture: more land is needed to farm and this land is farmed more intensively leaving it little time to recover. In forest areas, this can result in a permanent loss of forest. Deforestation causes soil deterioration, which can lead to soil erosion. Over the centuries, deforestation has removed most of the **rainforest** in Madagascar and now only a few fragments remain.

**desertification** A process of land degradation in which previously fertile land can be turned into barren land or desert. It is usually caused by **drought** or the overuse of fragile lands. Desertification only occurs in drylands, which have low, infrequent, and irregular rainfall and high temperatures. In Southern Africa, this includes the fringes of the Namib Desert and the semidesert Kalahari.

**Difaqane** A Sotho-Tswana word meaning "scattering." It is used to refer to the period (1819–39) of mass migrations and wars in the southeastern half of Southern Africa. The Difaqane was triggered by the rise of the Zulu kingdom. This period is known as the **Mfecane** by the Nguni peoples east of the Drakensberg Mountains.

**disenfranchisement** Depriving a person of the right to vote or other rights of citizenship.

**divination** A common feature of many African religions, divination is practiced by **diviners** who use various tools (such as wooden figures, plants, bones, or seeds) to divine the spiritual cause of a specific problem such as illness, accident, or misfortune.

**diviner** A practitioner of **divination**.

**domba** In Venda society, girls who have completed the **vhusha** initiation process attend a school known as the domba to learn the duties expected of wives and mothers. Domba can also refer to the process of initiation itself.

**drought** Water shortage caused by a prolonged period of inadequate rainfall. Drought can have a devastating affect on the land and people who make their living from the land, in particular reducing the number of people following **nomadic** ways of life.

**durra** An alternative name for the cereal sorghum.

**electric mbira** A contemporary African style of music that translates the sounds of the **mbira** into guitar riffs accompanied by complicated drum patterns and vocals based on traditional singing styles.

**emahiya** A brightly-colored body wrap worn by Swazi men and women.

**fez** A brimless felt hat shaped like a truncated cone.

**Gaua** An evil god of some Khoisan religions, also called Gawama, who tries to disrupt the work of **Nadi**.

**Gawama** see Gaua

**granary** A building or room in which grain is stored.

**groundnut** A group of plants including the peanut, which is a major cash crop and food item in many African countries.

**hazomanga** A village ritual post used by the Sakalava.

**homeland** Usually meaning the land or country in which one lives or was born, it also refers to the South African Bantustans. Created by the South African government during the **apartheid** era, these were artificial homelands in which Black African peoples were forced to live. They often bore no relation to the areas in which groups had historically been associated with. The ten homelands were created from 260 "native reserves" that had been in existence since 1913. Homeland facilities and infrastructure were poor and their inhabitants suffered from overcrowding and poverty.

**hunter-gatherers** People who live off food that can be hunted or collected from the wild and do not cultivate crops or raise livestock.

**imzi** A Zulu homestead.

**Incwala** A three-week-long period, also called the First Fruits Festival, when the king and nation of Swaziland reaffirm their relationship.

**indlu** The basic social unit in Swazi society is the indlu (a husband and wife and their children). Several indlu make up an **umuti**. The members of an **umuti** share agricultural tasks.

**inkosi** Historically, the Xhosa's allegiance was to their **clan**, led by an inkosi whose status was gained through his mother. Inkosi (which actually means "thank-you") were obliged to be hospitable and generous and their powers were limited by public opinion and counselors.

**iscathamiya** An **a cappella** Zulu singing style originally from the all-male workers' hostels of 1920s Natal.

**Ismailis** A Muslim subsect that has as its spiritual leader the Aga Khan. The Ismailis believe that the office of Imam (leader) should have gone to a descendant of Ismail (died 760) when Jafar the sixth Imam died in 765.

**iwisa** A knobkerrie – a stick with a round knob at the end – used as a club or missile by Zulu warriors.

**Jit Jive** A term coined by the internationally-successful Zimbabwean group, the Bhundu Boys. It is an energetic dance music featuring **mbira**-style guitars.

**kabosy** A Madagascan instrument similar to a guitar.

**kgotla** A Sotho-Tswana term that can be used to mean both meeting place and court.

**kia** A trancelike state that Kung healers usually achieve by performing a dance. This activates **num** (an energy from the gods), which is then used as a healing force.

**Koran** The sacred book of Islam.

**lamba** A wraparound dress that is a very traditional style of Madagascan clothing rarely worn today.

**lifela** Sotho songs describing the life of migrant laborers.

**lineage** An extended family that shares a common ancestor. If descent is traced through the male line, then the lineage is patrilineal. If descent is traced through female relatives, then the lineage is matrilineal. Groups of several related lineages are often organized into **clans**.

**lithoko** Sotho poetry praising a noble person.

**lobola** The name used by many Bantu-speaking people of Southern Africa for **bridewealth**.

**lolwapa** A low-walled courtyard that lies at the heart of a Tswana **compound**.

**mapoto** A beaded apron worn by a married Ndebele woman.

**marabi** An early form of **township** jazz based around three chords.

**matano** Made from clay or wood, matano figures are used to illustrate the stories and **milayo** that are part of the teaching process of Venda girls undergoing initiation.

**matrilineal** *see* **lineage**

**mbaqanga** A vocal style that can be traced back to the four-part harmonies of 1950s African-American bands. South African musicians at first copied these harmonies, but then added an extra voice, creating a five-part harmony style reminiscent of African singing.

**mbira** A musical instrument used by many people in Africa but particularly associated with the Shona. It consists of tuned metal strips attached to a resonating box. The mbira is also called the thumb piano.

**Mfecane** The Nguni word meaning "crushing." It is used to refer to the period (1819–39) of mass migrations and wars in the southeastern half of Southern Africa. The Mfecane was triggered by the rise of the Zulu kingdom. It is known as the **Difaqane** by the Sotho-Tswana people west of the Drakensberg Mountains.

**mhondoro** In the Shona religion, the ancestral spirits of influential people. Mhondoro spirits provide the link between mortals and god.

**milayo** A Venda saying that expresses a wise or clever observation or a general truth or belief.

**Mkhulumnqande** The creator-god of the Swazi religion.

**Molimo** The creator-god of the Tswana religion.

**mosque** A Muslim place of worship.

**mpsikidy** A Madagascan **diviner**.

**mudzimo** The ancestral spirit of an ordinary person according to the Shona religion.

**murundu** A **circumcision** ceremony for boys entering adulthood in Venda society.

**Murungu** see **Mwari**

**Mwari** The supreme god of the Shona religion, referred to as **Murungu** in historical documents.

**Nadi** The supreme god of some Khoisan religions.

**n'anga** Religious and medical practitioners of the Shona religion, who both heal illnesses with herbs and diagnose evil forces at work through **divination**.

**ndilo** A bowl used in the past for **divination** at the courts of Venda chiefs, in particular to identify witches.

**Ndlovukazi** The title of mother of the Swazi king; it literally means "Lady Elephant," a reference to her considerable influence and power.

**ngoma** A Venda drum played at a chief's court.

**ngozi** In the Shona religion, harmful ancestral spirits that are thought to cause evil; they can be the spirits of people who were murdered.

**Ngwenyama** The title of the Swazi king; it literally means "Lion."

**nomad** Used to describe people who follow a nomadic lifestyle. Nomads are "wanderers" (the word derives from "nomas," Latin for "wandering shepherd"), but they usually travel well-used paths, and their movements are dictated by the demands of trade or the needs of their herds for pasture and water.

**nomadic** Characteristic of, or like, **nomads** and their ways of life.

**num** *see* **kia**

**nyangas** Male herbalists in the Ndebele religion.

**ocher** A yellow or reddish-brown clay. Many people use ocher to color and style their hair or paint their bodies.

**omakipa** Ivory clasp-buttons that were given by an Ovambo bridegroom to his bride in the past.

**oruzo** In Herero society, a **lineage** that is traced through a person's male relatives.

**ozonganda** A Herero **compound**.

**pastoralism** Used to describe the lifestyle of a **pastoralist**.

**pastoralist** A person who raises livestock.

**pitsos** Sotho term for public meetings.

**protectorate** A state or territory that is controlled by a usually stronger nation. In particular it is used to refer to the colonies established by Europeans in Africa. African rulers were sometimes misled, forced, or tricked into signing protectorate treaties on the understanding that they were only a promise by the Europeans to protect their country from aggression, but were not told that the agreement gave them (the Europeans) sovereignty over their lands.

**rainforest** Dense forest found in tropical areas with heavy rainfall. The trees are nearly all broadleaved evergreens, such as ironwood and mahogany. Rainforests are ecologically very rich and house a greater variety of flora and fauna than most other environments.

**rumbira** A contemporary style of Zimbabwean music that blends **electric mbira** with Zairean rumba rhythms.

**sangoma** A Nguni word for a **diviner** or prophet. "Sangoma" literally means "people of the drum."

**sari** The main outer garment worn by Indian women, consisting of a long piece of cloth worn wrapped around the body with one end forming an ankle-length skirt and the other end draped over one shoulder.

**savanna** Flat, open grassland, usually with scattered bushes or trees, characteristic of much of tropical Africa.

**scrub** Dense vegetation consisting of stunted trees, bushes, and other plants. Sometimes referred to as bush.

**seminomadic pastoralism** A form of **pastoralism** involving the seasonal movement of livestock.

**Shiite** A member of one of the two main branches of Islam, Shiites regard Muhammad's son-in-law Ali and his descendants as the true Imams (leaders).

**shikuki** Ovambo reed baskets used for catching fish.

**sibhaca** A Swazi dance performed by men.

**sisal** A strong durable fiber made from leaves of the sisal plant; it is used to make rope, baskets, and other goods.

**sikidy** A form **divination** practiced in Madagascar.

**subsistence agriculture** A type of farming in which all or most of the crop is consumed by the farmer and his family leaving little or nothing to be marketed.

**Sunni** One of the two main branches of Islam, it consists of those who accept the authority of the Sunna. Sunnis make up about ninety percent of all Muslims.

**tinkhundla** Local authorities in Swaziland based on small groups of chieftaincies. In 1978, the Swazi king revived parliament (which he had previously dissolved in 1973) with a system of indirect, nonparty elections based on tinkhundla. This system allows the king to preserve his hold on power.

**townships** Government-built towns in South Africa that were created during the **apartheid** era to house people evicted from "white" towns. Townships often had poor facilities and high population levels. As their inhabitants' labor was still needed in the "white" towns, however, the government developed "subsidized busing" to take people from the townships to their place of work. The journey could take up eight hours and could cost a person a quarter of their wages.

**trekboer** A migrant Afrikaner farmer. Trekboers led the colonization of areas inland from the Cape in the 1700s.

**tumellano** Sotho songs in which groups of people sing together in harmony.

**Umhlanga** Every September in Swaziland, unmarried girls perform the Umhlanga, or Reed Dance, to pay homage to the queen mother.

**umnumzana** Each Swazi **umuti** has as its head an umnumzana, who is usually male but can be a woman. The umnumzana settles disputes, allocates land, and organizes workers.

**umuti** *see* **indlu**

**underemployment** A situation in which although few people are totally unemployed many do not have enough work to provide for their needs. For example, this can mean that a person may have a few part-time, low-paid jobs that do not fully exploit their potential.

**vako-drazana** Traditional Madagascan songs.

**vakojazzana** A contemporary Madagascan music style that combines jazz with **vako-drazana**.

**valiha** A Madagascan horn consisting of a long tube (in the past, it was usually of bamboo) with twenty or more strings stretched lengthwise around its circumference.

**vhusha** In Venda society, girls who have reached puberty undergo the six-day vhusha initiation process.

**Voortrekker** An Afrikaner who took part in the Great Trek (1836–45).

**zimbabwe** A dry-wall (without mortar) stone house or enclosure built by the Shona. The Shona probably began building zimbabwes in the late 1100s.

# Index

Peoples pages and special features are printed in **bold**; *italic* page numbers refer to illustrations, captions, or maps.

**A**

Abdullah Ibrahim (Dollar Brand) 62
African National Congress (ANC) 33, 40, *41*, 49, 99
Afrikaans language 33–34, *36*, 42, 50, 104
Afrikaans literature 35
Afrikaners 28, 29, **30–35**, 36, *36*, 37, 79, 87, 99, 103
  distribution of 24
  *see also* Boers
Afroasiatic languages 105, *105*
Age-regiments 82, 89, *102*
Agriculture 6, 44, 50, 59–60, 70, 73, 74, 76, 80, 83, 88, 91, 100
  *see also* Farming
Ambo *see* Ovambo language
Andrianampoinimerina *57*
Anglo-Boer War 32, *33*, *34*, 36, *36*
  Mafeking banknote *18*
Antaifasy people *56*
Antaimoro people *56*
Antaisaka people *56*
Antambahoaka people *56*
Antandroy people *56*
Antankarana people *56*
Antanosy people *56*, *59*
Apartheid 6, *20*, *21*, 29, **36–41**, 62–63, *63*
  Afrikaners 32, 33, 34, *35*, 36, *36*, 37, 39
  Cape Coloreds and Cape Malays 42, 43
  Herero people 46
  Indian South Africans 49, *49*, 50–51
  Ovambo people 68, 69
  Sotho people 79, *81*
  Tswana people 87
  Venda people 91, 93
  Xhosa people 95, 96
  Zulu people 99
Arabic language 59, 104, *105*
Arabs 42, 59, 61, 77
Area of countries 6
Asiatic Land Tenure Act 49
AWB (Afrikaner Weerstandsbeweging) *35*

**B**

Bantu Education Act 38
Bantu languages *104*, 105
Bantu-speaking peoples 26, 28, 31, 53, 64, 70, 72, 78, 82, 86, 90, 94, 98
Bantustans *see* Homelands
Bapedi Empire 79
Bara people *56*
Basotho *see* Sotho people
Basuto Kingdom 79, *79*
Batswana *see* Tswana people
Beadwork 65, *66*, *67*, 70, *80*, *81*, *95*, 100, *101*
Betsileo people 56, *56*, *59*, 57
Betsimisaraka kingdom 57
Betsimisaraka people *56*, 57, *60*
Bezanozano people *56*
Bhundu Boys 63
Biko, Steve *40*
Black Consciousness *40*
Blood River, Battle of 32, *32*

Boers *17*, 27, 31, *34*, 53, 65, 83, *83*, 91, 95
  *see also* Afrikaners
Bokwe, John Knox 97
Bophuthatswana homeland 86, 87
Botha, Louis 36
Botswana
  area, GNP, population 6
  colonialism and independence 21
  distribution of peoples *24*
  location on map *5*, *7*
Breytenbach, Breyten 35
Bridewealth 97, 100
Brink, André 35
British South Africa Company 65
Broederbond 37
Buildings *43*, *46*, 47, *47*, *51*, *58*, *59*, *60*, *70*, 76, *76*, 77, *81*, 87, *87*, 88, *89*, *99*
Bushmen 52
Buthelezi, Chief *21*, *38*, 41, 99

**C**

Cape Colored people **42–43**, 53
  distribution of *24*
Cape of Good Hope *16*, 27, 30
Cape Malay people **42–43**
  distribution of *24*
Cape-Xhosa wars 95
Caprivi Strip 8
Cash crops 60, 66, 67, 74, 83, 92
Caste system, Hindu 51
Cattle 26, 27, *31*, 44, 45, 46–47, 53, 55, *55*, 60, 70, 80, 83, 88, 89, 90, 95, 97
Central Kalahari Game Reserve 54
Cetshwayo 99
Chimurenga 63
Chinese people 42, 56, 59, 60
Chiweshe, Stella 63
Christianity 29
  Herero people 47
  Indian South Africans 51
  Madagascan peoples 58, 61
  Ndebele people 67
  Ovambo people 71
  Shona people 75
  Sotho people 81
  Swazi people 85
  Tswana people 89
  Venda people 93
  Xhosa people 97
  Zulu people 101
Chronologies
  events to 1848 16–17
  events 1851–1967 18–19
  events 1972 – present day 20–21
Ciskei homeland 95
"Click" languages 54, 63
  *see also* Khoisan languages
Climate 10–11
Clothing *45*, *47*, *51*, *57*, *84*, *95*
Coastal lowlands 9, 27
Coldstream Stone *54*
Colonialism 21, *23*, 27, 29, 32, 36, 45, *50*, 57–58, 69, 73, 74, 79, 83, 87, 89, 91, 103
Color bars 38
Communist Party of South Africa 33
Comorans 56, 61
Comoros Islands 56
  area, GNP, population 6

colonialism and independence 21
  location on map *5*, *7*
Concentration camps, British 32, *33*
"Cullinan" Diamond *18*

**D**

Defiance Campaign 37, *39*, 40
Deserts 27
  vegetation 12
  wildlife 15
Desertification 28
Diago, Beulah 63
Dias, Bartholomeu *16*
Difaqane *see* Mfecane/Difaqane
Dingiswayo 98, 102
Divination 61, *61*, 67, 85, *91*, 93, 101
Division of labor 47, 55, 60, 70, 80, 84, 88
Dlamini I 82
Dollar Brand 62
Drakensberg Mountains 10, 27, 78, 102, 103
Drums and drumming *92*, *93*
Dube, John L. 40
Dutch East India Company 30, 42
Dutch Reformed Church 29, 35, 43

**E**

Elifas, Filemon 69
Emilien, Jean 63
Epstein, Sir Jacob *58*
Escarpment, Great 8, 9
Ethnic groups
  definition 5
  distribution 24–25
  population figures 28

**F**

Farming 27, 29, 36, 43, 60, 66–67, 78, 83, 88, 100
  *see also* Agriculture
Figurines *58*, *73*, *75*, *92*, *100*
Forces Vives 59
Forests
  vegetation 13
  wildlife 14
Front-line states 39
Furniture *74*, *84*, *100*

**G**

Gandhi, Mohandas Karamchand 40, 49, *49*
Gcaleka Xhosa people 94
Geography of Southern Africa
  climate 10–11
  land 8–9
  overview 27–28
  vegetation 12–13
  wildlife 14–15
GNP of countries 6
Goodwill, King Zwelethini 100
Great Trek 27, 31, *31*, *32*, 36, 65
Great Zimbabwe 27, 73, *73*, 74, 75, **76–77**
Griqua people 65
Group Areas Act 38
Gujarati language 50

**H**

Hairstyles *59*, *83*, *84*
Headdresses *45*, *53*, *95*, *96*, *101*
Headrests *74*, *84*, *100*
Herero language 46, *104*
Herero massacre 45, *45*, 46

Herero people **44–47**, 53
  distribution of 24
  Ovambo people and 44, 68
Herero religion 47
Hertzog, J. B. M. *36*, 37
Hindi language 50
Hindu religion 51
History of Southern Africa
  chronologies 16–21
  overview 26–27
  pictorial 22–23
Hlubi Xhosa people 94
Homelands 29, 38, *38*, 46, 66, 79,
  82, 86, 87, 91, 93, 95, 96–97, 99
Homesteads *97*, *99*
Hottentot Code 38
Hottentots 52
Huguenots (French Protestants) 30
Hunter-gatherers 26, 52, 54
"Hut-tax" disks *23*

**I**
Indian people 28, 42, 56, 59, 60
Indian South Africans 37, **48–51**
  distribution of 24
Initiation *80*, *83*, *92*, 93, *93*, *96*
Inkatha Freedom Party (IFP) 41, 99
International Defense and Aid Fund *39*
Iscathamiya 62, *62*
IsiNdebele *see* Ndebele language
IsiXhosa *see* Xhosa language
IsiZulu *see* Zulu language
Islam 104
  Cape Malays 43, *43*
  Indian South Africans 51, *51*
  Madagascan peoples 61

**J**
Jazz, South African 62–63, *63*
Jit Jive 63

**K**
Kalahari Desert 28, 45, 54, 73
  vegetation 12, 13
KaNgwane homeland 82
Kaokoveld Plateau 44, 47, *47*
Khama, Sir Seretse 87
Khoikhoi people *31*, *36*, 39, 42, 52–53, 54
  *see also* Khoisan people
Khoisan languages 54, 105, *105*
  sign language *55*
Khoisan people 26, 28, **52–55**, 78, 94
  distribution of 24
  rock art *16*, *55*
Khoisan religions 54, 55
Khumalo Ndebele people 65, 103
Khwe Khoisan people 54
Kora people 65
Kruger, Paul *35*
Krugerrand *18*
Kung Khoisan people *54*
Kung language *105*
KwaNdebele homeland 66
KwaZulu homeland 99
Kwena (Crocodile) clan 79

**L**
Ladysmith Black Mambazo 62, *62*
Lakes 9

wildlife 15
Land 8–9
Land Rights Bill 80
Languages 28–29, 33–34, 42, 46,
  50, 54, *55*, 59, *63*, 66, 70 ,73,
  80, 83, 87, 91, 96, 99, **104–105**
Lebowa homeland 79
Lembede, Anton 40
Lesotho
  area, GNP, population 6
  colonialism and independence 21
  distribution of peoples *24*
  location on map *5*, *7*
Letsie III, King 80
Limpopo River 9, 26, 27, 86, 90, 91
Luvenda language 91, *104*

**M**
Mabhogo, King 65
Madagascan peoples **56–61**
  distribution of 25
  list and locations of *56*
Madagascar 26, 28
  area, GNP, population 6
  colonialism and independence 21
  distribution of peoples *25*
  location on map *5*, *7*
  vegetation 13
  wildlife 15
Mahafaly people *56*, *58*, 61
Maherero, Samuel 45
Makeba, Miriam *63*
Makoa people *56*
Malagasy language 59, 104
Malagasy religion 61
Malagasy Republic 59
Malan, Dr Daniel François *36*, 37
Malayo-Polynesian people 26, 28, 42, 57
Manala Ndebele people 64, 65
Mandela, Nelson 6, *39*, 40, 41, *41*, 96
Mapfumo, Thomas *62*, 63
Mapungubwe, gold rhinoceros from *16*
Marriage 43, 51, 55, 60–61, 67,
  75, 84, 89, 95, 97, 100
Masekela, Hugh 62, *63*
Masire, Sir Ketumile 87
Matabele people 26, 27, **64–67**
  distribution of 25
Mauritius
  area, GNP, population 6
  colonialism and independence 21
  location on map *5*, *7*
Mbaqanga 62, *63*
Mbira *62*, 63
Merina kingdom 57, *57*
Merina people *56*, 57, 58 ,*59*
Metalworking 71, 78, 100
Mfecane/Difaqane *17*, 26, 27, 73, 77, 79,
  *79*, 83, 87, 98, **102–103**
Migrant labor 29, 70, 80, 84, 87, 92, 100
Mining *23*, 29, 36, 37, 38, 74, 80, 84,
  88–89, 92, 96, 100
Ministry of Native (Bantu) Affairs 37, *37*
Mokhehle, Dr Ntsu 80
Moshoeshoe I 79, *79*, 103
Moshoeshoe II 80
Mosque, Soofie *51*
Mozambique

area, GNP, population 6
colonialism and independence 21
distribution of peoples 24–25
location on map *5*, *7*
Mpondo Xhosa people 94
Mswati I 82, 83, *83*
Mthethwa kingdom 98, 102, *102*, *103*
Mthethwa people 102
Mugabe, Robert *20*, 66
Mural art *67*
Musi, Chief 65
Music 35, **62–63**, *92*, *93*
Muslims *see* Islam
Mutota, Nyatsimba 73, *73*
Mwene Mutapas 73
Mzilikazi 65, 103

**N**
Namib Desert 10, 28
  vegetation 12
  wildlife 14
Namibia
  area, GNP, population 6
  colonialism and independence 21
  distribution of peoples *24*
  location on map *5*, *7*
  South African occupation 6, 39, 46, 53, 69
Natal Indian Congress 49
Natalia republic 32, *32*
National Party (NP) 32, 34, 36, 37, 38, 49
Native Land Act 37
"Native reserves" 37, 46, 91
Ndebele kingdom 103
Ndebele language 66, *104*
Ndebele people 26, 27, **64–67**
  distribution of 25
Ndebele religion 67.
Ndwandwe kingdom 102, *102*
Ndwandwe people 102
Ndzundza Ndebele people 64, 65
Ngoni peoples 26, 103, *103*
Ngqika Xhosa people 94
Nguni peoples 26, 64–65, 77, 82, 94, 98, 102
Ngwane II 82
Ngwane kingdom 82, 102, *102*, 103
Ngwane people 82, 102, 103
Niger-Kordofanian languages *104*, 105
Nilo-Saharan languages *104*, 105
Nkomo, Joshua 66
Nkosi Dlamini clan 84
Nomadism *47*, 54
Nongqawuse 95
Northern Sotho language *104*

**O**
Ojitherero *see* Herero language
Okavango Swamps 9, 15, 27, 86
Orange Free State (republic) 32, *32*, 79
Ovahimba Herero people 47, *47*
Ovambo language 70, *104*
Ovambo people **68–71**
  distribution of 24
  Herero people and 44
Ovambokavango Church 71

**P**
Pan-Africanist Congress (PAC) 40
Pass Laws 38–39, *39*
Pastoralism 26, 53, 54

# Index

Pedi Sotho people 79
Peoples of Southern Africa
  distribution of 24–25
  introduction 26–29
  today 6–7, 28–29
Pipes 81, 95
Plaatje, Sol 40
Ponies, Basotho 79
Population 6
  density 7
  ethnic groups 28
  major towns 7
Population Registration Act 38, 43
Pottery 71, 75, 77, 91, 96
Python dance 93

**R**
Radama I, King 57–58, 57
Railroads, major 6
Rainfall 10–11
Rainforests 26, 28
  vegetation 13
  wildlife 15
Ramanantsoa, General Gabriel 58–59
Ranavalona I, Queen 57, 58
Ranavalona II, Queen 58
Randimbiarison, Ricky 63
Ratsimandrava, Colonel Richard 59
Ratsimilaho 57
Ratsiraka, Didier 59
Ravahiny, Queen 57
Ravony, Francisque 59
"Red" Xhosa 97
Religions 29, 47, 51, 55, 61, 67,
  75, 81, 85, 89, 93, 97, 101
  see also Christianity, Islam
Retief, Piet 31
Rhinoceros, gold 16
Rhodes, Cecil 23, 65, 73
Rift Valley, Great 9, 27
Rivers 9
  wildlife 15
Roads, major 6
Rock art, Khoisan 16, 55
Rozvi Empire 73
Rozvi Shona people 73

**S**
Sakalava kingdom 57
Sakalava people 56, 58, 59, 61
San people 52, 53, 54
  see also Khoisan people
Sangomas 67, 101
Savannas 27
  vegetation 13
  wildlife 15
"School" Xhosa 97
Seashore, wildlife 15
Semideserts 12, 15, 27
Separate Amenities Act 37
Sesotho language 80, 104
Sesotho sa Leboa see Northern
  Sotho language
Setswana language 87, 104
Shaka 17, 65, 73, 95, 98, 101, 102, 102, 103
Sharpeville massacre 40, 41
Shona language 28, 73, 104

Shona people 26, **72–75**
  distribution of 25
  see also Great Zimbabwe
Shona religion 75
Sihanaka people 56
Sikh soldier 50
Sinxo 97
Sisulu, Walter 40
SiSwazi see Swazi language
Slavery 36, 42, 91
Snuff boxes 96, 99
Sobhuza I 83, 102
Sobhuza II 83
Soofie Mosque 51
Sotho literature, oral 81
Sotho people 26, 27, 64, **78–81**,
  86–87, 102, 103
  distribution of 25
Sotho reiglion 81
South Africa 26, 27
  area, GNP, population 6
  distribution of peoples 24
  front-line states and 39
  location on map 5, 7
  occupation of Namibia 6, 39, 46, 53, 69
  see also Apartheid
South African Native National Congress 40
South African Republic (Transvaal) 32, 91
South West Africa People's Organization
  (SWAPO) 19, 46, 69
Southern Africa
  introduction 26–29
  today 6–7
Southern Plateau 27
Soutpansberg republic 91
Soweto uprisings 41
Swahili ports 77
Swati see Swazi language
Swazi kingdom 27, 82, 103
Swazi language 83, 104
Swazi people 26, **82–85**, 90, 98
  distribution of 25
Swazi religion 85
Swaziland
  area, GNP, population 6
  colonialism and independence 21
  distribution of peoples 24
  location on map 5, 7

**T**
Tambo, Oliver 40
Tamil language 50
Tanala people 56
Tarika 63
Telugu language 50
Temperature 10–11
Terre' Blanche, Eugene 35
Thandile, Queen Regent 82, 85
Thembu Xhosa people 94, 96
Thoho ya Ndou 90
Thumb pianos 62, 63
Tombs 58, 61, 61
Tourism 60, 79, 84
Townships 40–41, 41, 62, 96
Trade 27, 29, 43, 53, 72, 76, 77
Transkei homeland 95
Transvaal Indian Congress 49
Treason Trial 39

Trekboers 31
Tshivenda see Luvenda language
Tsimihety people 56
Tsiranana, Philibert 58
Tsitambala confederation 57
Tsonga people 26
Tswana people 26, 79, 81,
  **86–89**, 102, 103
  distribution of 24
Tswana religion 81, 89
Tutu, Desmond 41

**U**
Umhlanga dance 85, 85
Umkonto we Sizwe 40, 41
Union of South Africa 19, 36, 65, 91
United Party 37
Urdu language 50

**V**
Valiha horn 63
Vazimba people 57
Vegetation 12–13
Venda homeland 91, 93
Venda language see Luvenda language
Venda literature, oral 93
Venda people 26, **90–93**
  distribution of 25
Venda religion 93
Verwoerd, Dr Hendrik 37
Vhalembba Venda people 90
Vhangona Venda people 90
Vhasenzi Venda people 90
Vhatavhatsindi Venda people 90
Vhavenda see Venda people
Voortrekker Monument 34
Voortrekkers 31, 32

**W**
Western Austronesian languages 59
Western Sotho see Tswana people
Wildlife 14–15
Winds 10

**X**
Xhosa language 96, 104
Xhosa literature 97
Xhosa people 17, 26, 31, **94–97**, 98
  distribution of 25
Xhosa religion 97

**Z**
Zafy, Professor Albert 59
Zimbabwe 26, 27
  area, GNP, population 6
  colonialism and independence 19, 20, 21
  distribution of peoples 24
  location on map 5, 7
Zimbabwes (buildings) 72, 76
  see also Great Zimbabwe
Zulu kingdom 27, 98, 102–103
Zulu language 50, 96, 99, 104
Zulu people 26, 31, 32, 32, 49, 62, 65, **98–101**
  battle formation 101
  distribution of 25
  warriors 17, 102
  weapons 101, 103
  see also Mfecane/Difaqane
Zulu religion 101
Zwide 102